A Handbook of Composers and their music

Paul Farmer

Oxford University Press
Music Department, Ely House, 37 Dover Street, London WIX 4AH

First published 1982
ISBN 0 19 321092 4

by the same author
Music in the Comprehensive School

Designed by Ann Samuel

Filmset and printed in Great Britain by
BAS Printers Limited, Over Wallop, Hampshire

Acknowledgements

Page 4 (top) Cooper-Bridgeman Library, by permission of Viscount de l'Isle, (bottom) British Library; p. 5 (left) National Portrait Gallery, (right) Mansell Collection; p. 7 Mander and Mitchenson Theatre Collection; p. 8 Mander and Mitchenson Theatre Collection; p. 10 Archiv für Kunst und Geschichte, Berlin (2); p. 11 British Library; p. 12 Archiv für Kunst und Geschichte, Berlin; p. 13 Mansell Collection (2); p. 14 (top) Mansell Collection, (bottom) Royal Academy of Arts; p. 15 Mansell Collection; p. 16 (top) Mansell Collection, (bottom) Archiv für Kunst und Geschichte, Berlin; p. 17 (top and bottom) Archiv für Kunst und Geschichte, Berlin, (centre) British Library; p. 19 (top and bottom) Archiv für Kunst und Geschichte, Berlin, (centre) Mansell Collection; p. 20 (top) Archiv für Kunst und Geschichte, Berlin, (bottom) British Library; p. 22 Illustrated London News; p. 24 (top) National Gallery, London, (bottom) Piano Publishers Association; p. 25 Electronic Music Studios Ltd; p. 27 (top) Theatre Museum, (bottom) Museum der Stadt Wien; p. 28 Beethovenhaus, Bonn; p. 29 Mansell Collection; p. 30 British Museum; p. 31 Archiv für Kunst und Geschichte, Berlin; p. 32 Zentral Bibliothek, Zürich; p. 33 (top) Mansell Collection, (bottom) Bildarchiv der Öst. Nationalbibliothek, Vienna; p. 34 (top) Archiv für Kunst und Geschichte, Berlin, (bottom) National Gallery, Berlin; p. 35 (left) Mansell Collection; p. 38 Bodleian Library, Oxford; p. 39 Mansell Collection; p. 40 Archiv für Kunst und Geschichte, Berlin (2); p. 43 (top) Illustrated London News, (left) Walter Danz, (right) BBC; p. 44 (left) Clive Barda, (top) Archiv für Kunst und Geschichte, Berlin; p. 45 Museo del Prado, Madrid; p. 46 Mansell Collection; p. 47 (top) H. Roger-Viollet; p. 50 (top) H. Roger-Viollet, (bottom) British Library; p. 51 (top) Photographie Bulloz, (bottom) Mansell Collection; p. 54 (top) Archiv für Kunst und Geschichte, Berlin, (bottom) Schumannhaus, Zwickau; p. 56 (top) Mansell Collection; p. 57 (top) British Library, (bottom) Bildarchiv der Öst Nationalbibliothek, Vienna; p. 59 (bottom) Radio Times Hulton Picture Library; p. 60 Archiv für Kunst und Geschichte, Berlin (2); p. 61 Radio Times Hulton Picture Library; p. 62 (left) Ferdinandeum Museum, Innsbruck; p. 63 Bettmann Archive, New York; p. 67 Richard Macnutt Collection; p. 68 Novosti Press Agency (2); p. 69 (top) Novosti Press Agency; p. 70 (bottom) Novosti Press Agency; p. 72 (left) Archiv für Kunst und Geschichte, Berlin, (right) Interfoto MTI, Budapest; p. 73 (left) Interfoto MTI, Budapest, (top) Radio Times Hulton Picture Library, (bottom) Archiv für Kunst und Geschichte, Berlin; p. 75 (top) Mansell Collection, (centre) Bettmann Archive, New York, (bottom) photo J. Heinrich; p. 78 (top) British Museum, (bottom) Collection de Mme de Tinan © SPADEM; p. 79 Collection de Mme de Tinan © SPADEM (2); p. 80 Bibliothèque Nationale; p. 81 Clive Barda (2); p. 82 (top) Kurt Hutton, (bottom) Nigel Luckhurst; p. 83 (top) Illustrated London News, (bottom) Grainger Museum, University of Melbourne; p. 84 (top) Fitzwilliam Museum, Cambridge, (bottom) Oxford University Press; p. 85 (left) Boosey & Hawkes Music Publishers Ltd., (right) Clive Barda; p. 86 (top) Artist's collection, (bottom) Radio Times Hulton Picture Library; p. 87 (bottom) Foto Piccagiani (Teatro alla Scala, Milan), (right) Boosey & Hawkes Music Publishers Ltd.; p. 89 (left) Culver Pictures, Inc., (right) CBS, New York; p. 90 Dancing Times; p. 91 (top) Universal Edition (London) Ltd., (bottom) Archiv für Kunst und Geschichte, Berlin (2); p. 92 (top) Alfred A. Kalmus (Universal Edition) Ltd., (bottom) Opernhaus Zürich © Susann Schimert-Ramme; p. 94 (bottom) Ralph Fassey; p. 95 (bottom) Eric Auerbach.

The author and publisher are grateful to Miss Esmé Burrough, Miss Thelma Manning, Mr. Alistair Salmond and Mrs. Jill Scarfe for commenting on the draft manuscript of this book and testing sections of it with their classes.

For Clare, Chloe, Anna and Polly

Contents

Teacher's note

The **Things to do** section at the end of each chapter has been specially written to cater for a variety of classroom needs, and contains activities suitable for pupils of different abilities and interests. In general these have been arranged as follows:

1. The first activity is always an essentially musical one, either involving the theory of music or practical work or both. Some of these activities are much more demanding than others, but the book as a whole contains enough of this kind of work to cover a wide range of abilities.

2. The second activity is usually one which does not involve much written work, (e.g. the making of charts, posters, etc.) and can be attempted regardless of 'academic' ability.

3. The final activity is useful as extension work for those pupils who are able and wish to research the subject further.

Elizabethan music

Queen Elizabeth I of England was born in 1533. She became Queen in 1558, and died in 1603; so we think of the **Elizabethan Age** as being the second half of the 16th century. At this time England was a leading musical country, and there were several English composers alive whose music is still played. The queen herself was also very interested in music.

Thomas Tallis (1505–1585) was organist of the **Chapel Royal** (this is the name for the Queen's own church musicians), and wrote a lot of church music. His **canon** (see *Things to do*, number 1a) is still regularly sung as a hymn tune. He also wrote a **motet** (an unaccompanied setting of religious words for voices) for eight choirs, each with five parts, called *Spem in Alium*. This piece has a total of forty separate voice parts!

One of Tallis's pupils was William Byrd (1543–1623). He was organist at Lincoln Cathedral and then at the Chapel Royal. He was a Catholic, at a time when many Catholics were persecuted in England, but somehow he was allowed to keep his religion. In fact he was

Queen Elizabeth I enjoyed music and dancing

so popular with Queen Elizabeth that she allowed him and Tallis to be the only people in the country who could print music.

During the reign of Queen Elizabeth a new type of music called the **madrigal** developed in England. This was written for several voices singing different parts. It was rather like a motet, except that it was not written for the church. In a way, it was one of the very earliest forms of popular song.

Thomas Morley (1557–1603) has been called 'the father of the English madrigal'. He was an organist of St Paul's Cathedral in London, and a 'Gentleman of the Chapel Royal' (this means he sung in the Chapel Royal). He must have also been popular with Queen Elizabeth, as he took over the monopoly of music printing from Tallis and Byrd. In 1597 he wrote a book called the *Plaine and Easie Introduction to Practicall Musicke*.

Another madrigal writer was Orlando Gibbons (1585–1625). He was also an organist of the Chapel Royal, and later of Westminster Abbey. He published only one volume of madrigals. One of them, *The Silver Swan*, is still

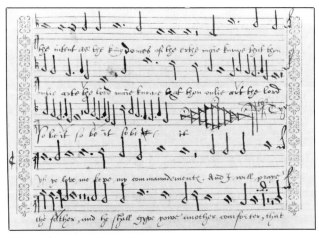
A manuscript of a piece of church music by Thomas Tallis

William Shakespeare, whose plays contain many songs and references to music

Making music in Elizabethan times. One lady sings, while the other two accompany her on the flute and lute

well known. Gibbons was one of the last of the madrigal composers, and after his death very few of these pieces were written.

William Shakespeare, the English playwright, lived at almost exactly the same time that Elizabeth I was on the throne. Like the queen, he was very interested in music. Not only are there many songs and references to music in his plays, but often his stage directions ask for music to be played. Most people went to the theatre in those days, and Shakespeare's plays gave many people the chance to enjoy music.

The composers in Queen Elizabeth's day wrote a lot of their music in what we call **variation** form. They wrote one short tune (an **air**), and then wrote it again in several different ways (the **variations**). They might make the variations higher or lower, or give them a different rhythm. Another popular form of composition was to put together two dance tunes to make one longer piece. Usually one of the tunes would be slow (such as a **pavan**), and the other would be quicker (such as the **galliard**).

Music was obviously an important part of Elizabethan life. People sang folk songs, or rounds and catches (these were like small canons—*Three Blind Mice* is an example); there were also madrigals, often sung by people connected with the aristocracy and the court; and there was a great deal of church music. There were also plenty of instruments to play this music on: the **virginals** (a small

harpsichord), small organs, **viols** (which looked like violins, but had frets like guitars), recorders (in different sizes), lutes, trumpets and drums.

After the Elizabethan composers and Henry Purcell (see page 7), England produced very few composers until the 19th century.

Questions

1 When was the **Elizabethan Age**?
2 Who was Thomas Tallis?
3 Which of Thomas Tallis's compositions has 40 voice parts?
4 Name and describe one of Tallis's pupils.
5 What is a **madrigal**?
6 Name two madrigal composers.
7 How do you think we know that Shakespeare was interested in music?
8 Explain in your own words what **Air and Variations** means.
9 Name and describe some of the instruments used in Elizabethan times.
10 How 'musical' a country was England in the 16th century? Explain your answer.

5

Things to do

1a Here is the beginning of Tallis's canon, the
well known hymn tune sung to the words
'Glory to Thee my God this Night'. In a
true canon all the parts sing the same tune,
one after the other, but in this extract the
alto part has harmony notes. Can you fill
in the missing tenor part? Copy the whole
extract into your book first.

1b Use any instruments to play Tallis's canon.
You will need two or more players:

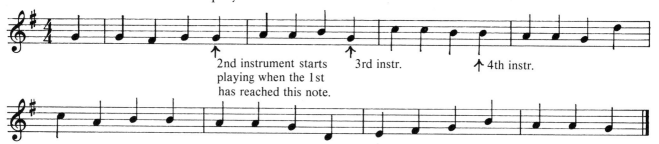

2nd instrument starts
playing when the 1st
has reached this note.

3rd instr.

4th instr.

2 Make a chart about Elizabethan
composers. First list the composers
mentioned in this chapter down the left
hand side of your page, and make four
vertical columns to the right of your list. In
these columns you can put: the dates each
composer lived; where they worked; the
names of any of their compositions; any
other important information.

3 Use a music reference book such as *The
Oxford Junior Companion to Music* to find out
all you can about the **Chapel Royal**.

Answer as many as you can of the
following questions about it:

a What exactly is the Chapel Royal? (It
really has two meanings.)

b How old is it?

c How were boys recruited to it during
Richard III's reign?

d Why was the Chapel Royal not used
for a time?

e Where does the Chapel Royal work
now?

Purcell (1659–1695)

Henry Purcell's father was a professional singer when Charles II returned to the English throne in 1660. Since church music was now sung once more (Oliver Cromwell had previously banned it) Henry's father was able to make a living as a church musician. So when he joined the choir of the Chapel Royal, it is not surprising that his son Henry also joined the choir as early as he could.

Henry did not just sing on Sundays, but spent all the week in the choir school, and learned all the usual school subjects. He also learned a lot of music, and was taught to play the lute, the violin and keyboard instruments (see page 23). There were also lessons in musical composition, and those pupils who were able could write **anthems** (accompanied settings of religious words for voices) which were sometimes performed by the choir.

The English composer Henry Purcell

Once Purcell's voice broke he could no longer sing. However, he stayed at the Chapel Royal where he did all sorts of jobs, from writing pieces of music which were needed very quickly, to looking after the King's instruments and tuning the organ. He possibly taught some of the younger boys as well.

A few years later Purcell suddenly became famous. In 1677 the composer Matthew Locke died, and Purcell was asked by the King to take over from Locke as composer for the King's string orchestra. This was a very important job for an 18-year-old. Two years later Purcell became organist at Westminster Abbey; this was not because the previous organist had died, but simply because the older man thought Purcell was better than he was, and wanted the young man to take over! These two jobs made Purcell the most important musician in the country.

Not surprisingly, Purcell's music soon began to be published. His two jobs meant that he had to write a lot of music. This tended to be rather serious for the Abbey, but lighter for the Chapel Royal or the Court, since the King seemed to enjoy lively music.

Purcell wrote many short pieces for all sorts of rather unimportant occasions, as well as other pieces for coronations and royal funerals. Like several other composers who followed him, Purcell died early, at the age of 37.

Purcell's music

Many of Purcell's pieces are written in what is called **binary form**, which means that they contain two different sections. Like many Elizabethan composers, Purcell also *combined* two short pieces, to make one longer piece. But he did rather more than just this, and often put *several* pieces together, to make up a **suite**. This was a collection of dances.

Purcell also wrote what could be described as a **bass with variations**. This is a piece where the same bass part is played over and over again, with a different tune above it each time. Probably one of the best known of all these **ground basses** (which is what we now call them) is *When I am Laid in Earth*, from his opera *Dido and Aeneas*. This tune is played at the Cenotaph each year on Remembrance Sunday.

Dido and Aeneas is one of Purcell's most popular pieces of music, and is still performed regularly. It was written for a girls' school in Chelsea, London, when Purcell was about 30. He wrote a lot of music for the theatre, including *King Arthur*, *The Fairy Queen* and *The Indian Queen* (these are very similar to operas) as well as music to accompany some of Shakespeare's plays (**incidental music**).

Purcell seems to have been a very adaptable composer. Not only did he write very serious music for the church, such as funeral anthems (for example, for Queen Mary, the wife of Charles II, when she died in 1694), but lots of short pieces to celebrate special occasions. The same Queen had birthday **odes** written for her on every birthday from her coronation to her death, and even the return of the King from some journey would be a good enough excuse to write a welcoming piece of music. Purcell's music, like that of many composers of that time, was very often 'tailor-made'.

Not only has much of Purcell's music lasted until the present day, but it was also a source of inspiration for the composer Benjamin Britten (see page 86).

The Duke's Theatre, Dorset Gardens, overlooking the River Thames. Many of Purcell's works for the theatre, including The Fairy Queen, *were first staged here*

Questions

1. What was Purcell's father's job?
2. What event in history took place the year after Purcell was born?
3. Why was this event (Q.2) important for Purcell's father?
4. Where did Purcell receive his first musical training?
5. Why did Purcell stop singing in the choir of the Chapel Royal?
6. What did Purcell do, once he stopped singing?

7   What two events suddenly made Purcell famous?
8   Explain why Purcell's music was sometimes serious and
    sometimes light.
9   Describe **binary form**.
10 Give some examples of Purcell's 'tailor-made' music.

Things to do

1   Next time you are asked by your teacher to make up some music
    of your own in class, try playing a **ground bass** with another
    instrument. Whoever has the lower instrument, such as a bass or
    alto xylophone, should play this line of music over and over
    again:

Ground bass

The higher instrument, such as a recorder, should make up
several tunes to go with this bass, using plenty of quavers. These
tunes should then be played one after the other while the bass is
repeated. Here are two tunes you can use to start with:

Tune 1

Tune 2

2   One of Purcell's favourite types of music was opera, or music for
    the theatre. Look through this book (especially the section on
    opera, page 62) and see which other composers have written
    operas, and then make a list of them all. Make your list into a
    chart or poster for your classroom wall, including dates and other
    information where you can.
3   Imagine that you are Purcell, aged about 11, and that you have
    just joined the choir at the Chapel Royal. Write one day's entry in
    a diary, just as the young Purcell might have done, describing
    some of the things that have happened to you: the services or
    practices you have sung at, the lessons you have had and the
    people you may have met.

Bach (1685–1750)

The German composer Johann Sebastian Bach

Johann Sebastian Bach was one of several composers who all had the same surname. They were in fact related to each other, but it is J. S. Bach who is usually considered the greatest of all the Bachs. He wrote such well known pieces as *Air on a G String*, the *48 Preludes and Fugues* and *Toccata and Fugue in D Minor*.

Bach was born at Eisenach, Germany, in 1685. This was the same year that another composer, George Frideric Handel was born (see page 13), though Handel lived nine years longer. Another difference between these two composers is that Handel travelled a great deal in his lifetime, and spent much of it outside Germany. Bach hardly travelled at all, and didn't even know much about his own country.

By the time Bach was ten years old his father and mother had both died, and he had to go to live with his elder brother who was an organist in a town not far away. Bach was sent to the local school, where he learnt all the usual subjects, while his brother taught him music. He also sung in the local church choir.

When Bach was fifteen he went to another school in a place called Luneberg, where he paid for his lessons by singing in the choir and later playing the violin in rehearsals. During the next few years he had a number of musical jobs in different towns, including Arnstadt, as an organist or director of music. All these different experiences of composing, arranging and performing music must have taught him a great deal about his subject. Like many composers of his time he was not *just* a composer, but also an all-round *musician*.

When he was 38, Bach moved to the city of Leipzig, where he became choirmaster at St Thomas's School. As well as training the singers, he had to compose a **cantata** (a religious piece of music for a choir) every Sunday for the singers to perform in one of the services of the city churches. He remained at Leipzig until he died in 1750, having reached quite an old age compared with many other composers.

Bach's first wife died, and so he re-married. Out of his 20 children only 11 lived to become adults. Three of the boys are still known for their own compositions, and one of them (J. C. Bach) taught Mozart for a short while (see page 19).

Bach's music

St. Thomas's Church, Leipzig, where Bach was choirmaster

Although Bach composed the equivalent of five cantatas for every Sunday in the year, only about 200 of them remain. Bach's importance as a composer is shown by the fact that these pieces which were originally written for church services are still performed today in concerts. Perhaps his best known pieces of church choral music are the St Matthew and St John **Passions** (these are the words of the gospels set to music), and the *Mass in B Minor* (the requiem service set to music).

As well as writing a great deal of choral music, Bach wrote a lot of music for the keyboard instruments of the time: **organ**, **harpsichord** and **clavichord**. Although the Preludes and Fugues for the organ are still played as they were originally intended on this instrument, the pieces for the other two instruments are now played on the piano—an instrument which had not been invented in Bach's time (see *Keyboard Instruments*, page 23).

A **Prelude** and **Fugue** were often written together. The Prelude was a kind of introduction, and was usually quite short. The Fugue was longer and, like a canon, all the parts came in one after the other. In each of the two books of Preludes and Fugues mentioned above, there were 24 of these pieces, making one piece for each of the major and minor keys. These pieces, which are very well known, are often just called 'the 48'.

Much of Bach's music is written in what is called **counterpoint.** This means that instead of the pieces being made up of blocks of notes (chords), there are many tunes (called **parts**) that are played at once. Many people would say that counterpoint is harder to compose than some chordal music, because there are so many tunes to think of which all have to fit together. Counterpoint can often be hard to play, too!

The manuscript of one of Bach's preludes from his famous collection of 48 Preludes and Fugues for keyboard

The opening of one of Bach's fugues, written in counterpoint. Compare it with the chordal music on page 36

J. S. Bach: Toccata in F sharp minor BWV 910

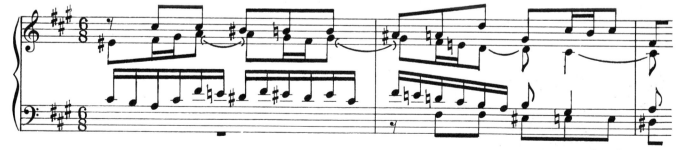

Questions

1 Which other well known composer was born in the same year as Bach?

2 How much longer than Bach did this other composer (Q.1) live?

3 What events changed Bach's life by the time he was ten?

4 Who first taught Bach music?

5 How did Bach pay for his lessons at the school in Luneburg?

6 What kind of jobs did Bach have during the next few years?

7 What was Bach's last job?

8 Describe Bach's duties in his last job.

9 Name and describe some of Bach's choral works.

10 Explain what is special about Bach's 48 Preludes and Fugues.

Things to do

1a Here is part of a fugue, in which all the parts play the same tune as they come in. One of the parts is missing, except for its first two notes. Copy out the whole extract in your book, and try to fill in the rest of the missing part. Remember that it uses the Bass clef:

1b Next time you make up some music in class, see if you can use the idea of a fugue. Whatever your music is like, try to get each instrument to imitate what the other has just played.

2 Make a chart of Bach's main compositions, using the information on the previous page. It could start like this:

Name of Piece	Description
295 cantatas	Pieces for church choirs
etc . . .	etc . . .

Make your chart as interesting as you can, if possible by adding your own handwritten copies of parts of Bach's music which your teacher may have.

3 Two differences between Bach and Handel are mentioned in this chapter. Read the next chapter about Handel, and then write a short passage which shows all the ways in which the two composers were different. Try to write about their music as well as their lives.

The organ Bach played at Arnstadt

Handel (1685–1759)

One thing that we can be fairly sure about is that George Frideric Handel was very keen on music when he was a small boy. There is a well known story about his being caught one night, practising the clavichord (a quiet keyboard instrument) in the attic of his house.

Handel had to be secretive about his practising because his father, who was a **barber-surgeon** (he shaved people and pulled teeth out) did not want him to get too interested in music. He wanted Handel to become a lawyer instead of a musician.

One day Handel's father took his son to stay with the boy's brother, who was servant to a duke about 40 miles from where Handel lived. The duke heard Handel playing, and was so impressed that he managed to persuade his father to pay for him to have proper music lessons. When Handel returned home to the town of Halle, he began his lessons with a man called Zachau. He was organist of the local cathedral, and taught George how to play the harpsichord, organ and violin, as well as how to compose.

When Handel was seventeen he went to study law at the local university, just as his father had wished. But he soon gave this up and went to Hamburg, a more exciting musical centre, where he got a job at the opera house. He spent the next few years in Italy, a very important country as far as music was concerned. He travelled around there and learned a lot about the Italian musical styles, especially opera.

When Handel returned to Germany, aged 25, he was appointed director of music to the Elector of Hanover. Soon after this he asked to go to London, and while there he wrote an opera, *Rinaldo*. The opera was performed in London and was most successful. After returning to Hanover for a while he went back to London again, only this time he stayed so long that the Elector got angry. So when Queen Anne died, and the Elector became George I of England, Handel got rather an unpleasant surprise. It was not until the *Water Music* was performed (see below) that the King forgave Handel, according to one story.

Handel stayed in London for the rest of his life, and spent most of his time working in the theatre. He wrote forty operas, but in spite of his success these eventually led him into debt, since operas were both expensive to stage and an unfashionable form of entertainment. It was because of his financial problems that he started to write oratorios (see next page).

The German composer George Frideric Handel

The inside of the church at Halle where Handel received his first music lessons

Handel's music

Handel's best known piece of music is *Messiah*, a large choral work for choir, orchestra and solo singers, which uses words from the Bible. It is thought that it only took Handel twenty-four days to write it. Another story is that when George II first heard the piece in London, he and all the audience were so impressed by the 'Hallelujah Chorus' that they stood up. Ever since then it has become a tradition to stand during this part of *Messiah*.

Messiah is an **oratorio**, a religious choral work which has no acting, and which can be performed in a church or theatre. Handel wrote several of these, mostly after his opera career had come to an end. It is strange to think that he might never have bothered writing *Messiah* if he had remained successful in the theatre for longer.

The *Water Music* is another well known composition by Handel. This was thought to have been written and played for George I, (the King who had previously quarrelled with Handel), on a state barge trip down the Thames. The story says that the King was so pleased with the music that it helped to mend their quarrel.

Since the composer J. S. Bach (see page 10) and Handel were born in the same year and the same country, it is natural to compare their music. Handel seems to have liked writing melodies for the human voice, perhaps because he had good professional singers available to perform his music. Bach, on the other hand, often gave his singers melodies which sound as if they might have been meant for instruments rather than voices. His music is often more complicated than Handel's, and seems rather like a musical jig-saw, with lots of different parts which all fit together.

Part of Handel's manuscript for the oratorio Messiah

Handel composed his Water Music *for a musical party on the Thames, rather like the one in this painting*

Questions

1 How do we know that Handel was interested in music when he was a small boy?
2 What did Handel's father want Handel to become?
3 What persuaded Handel's father to arrange music lessons for the boy?
4 What subject did Handel study at University?
5 Where did Handel travel and study during his early 20s?
6 Why did the Elector of Hanover get angry with Handel?
7 What piece of music is supposed to have ended George I's quarrel with Handel?
8 What sort of music did Handel first write in London? What made him change?

9 What story is told about the first performance of *Messiah*?
10 Describe the differences between the music of Bach and Handel.

Things to do

1a The opening bars of the *Hallelujah Chorus* are printed below. The
word Hallelujah (pronounced *hallylooya*) is separated in the
music, like this: Hal - le - lu - jah. If you are able to listen to a
recording of these opening bars, see if you can fill in the words,
just as they fit the music. You could copy the music into your book first:

1b Make up some music of your own, using the same *rhythm* as the
first bars of the *Hallelujah Chorus*. You could simply start with a
drum or tambourine playing the rhythm over and over again:

Next, try adding pairs of minims to this, played on other
instruments. Finally, see if you can add a tune, using crotchets.

2 The first London performance of *Messiah* was in the Theatre
Royal, Covent Garden. Tickets were 10s/6d, 5s or 3s/6d, and the
theatre opened at 4pm. Design your own advertisement for this
concert, as it might have looked at the time. How much do you
think the tickets would cost today?

3 EITHER imagine how both Handel and George I felt when they
came face to face in London, and write an imaginary account of
what happened in the form of a short sketch or newspaper
report; OR start your own project on **Royal Music**, beginning
with Handel's *Royal Fireworks Music*.

*Handel's Fireworks Music was
written for a special fireworks display
in Green Park, London, 1749, to
mark the signing of an important
peace treaty*

Haydn (1732–1809)

The Austrian composer Franz Joseph Haydn

Franz Joseph Haydn was born in a small town in Austria, near the border with Hungary, and lived with his family in a small thatched house. Haydn's father, who was a wheelwright, was not able to afford music lessons for Joseph or his brother Johann, who also became a composer. However, Joseph had a good treble voice which the choirmaster of a Viennese cathedral noticed on a visit to the town. As a result, Joseph, and later Johann, attended the cathedral choir school where they received a very good musical education.

As soon as a boy's voice broke he was no longer any use to the choir, and was usually sent away to earn his living in any way he could. This happened to Haydn just before he was 17. He was left on his own in Vienna, and might have very quickly become too poor to continue his interest in music. But somehow he managed to hire an attic, buy an old clavichord (see page 23) and make a little money from giving music lessons. In many towns or cities he probably wouldn't have been able to survive in this way; but Vienna was a very musical place, and there were quite a few people interested enough in music to become his pupils.

Haydn also wrote some music for the Viennese street bands, and one day he was noticed by someone who asked him to write an opera. By the time Haydn was 23 he was fortunate in having been employed as music director to two local noblemen at their country houses. There he would write pieces of music for their resident musicians to play. While he was employed by the second of these men he married a barber's daughter. She unfortunately turned out to be a most unsuitable wife (she is supposed to have used his music for curling her hair!) and so he made sure he saw her as little as possible.

In 1761, when Haydn was 29, he was appointed to a very important job as deputy music director to one of the richest noblemen in Austria, Prince Paul Esterházy. Five years later Haydn succeeded

Vienna in Haydn's time

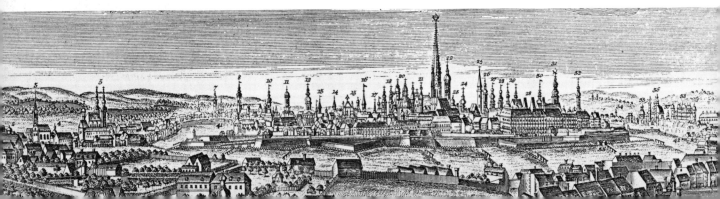

the principal director, and continued to serve Nicholas Esterházy, the brother of Paul. It was here that Haydn composed a lot of instrumental music for some of the best performers in the land; this gave him plenty of opportunity to perfect his compositions. He also became even better known outside Austria, for there were many visitors to the Esterházy residence.

In 1790 Prince Nicholas died, and Haydn retired with a pension. He was now free to compose how and where he liked. He made two successful visits to England, where he was very popular and composed the well known 'London' symphonies. He wrote his final compositions in Vienna before he died in 1809.

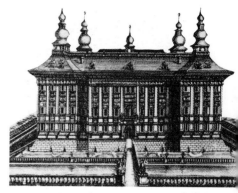

The Palace of Eisenstadt in Vienna—the Esterházy family's main residence

Haydn's music

Haydn used to be called 'the father of the symphony', because he developed the earliest symphony (which was just a few movements put together rather casually) into a complete musical whole. He also helped to develop **sonata form** (see page 40) and used it in his symphonies.

Haydn wrote over 100 symphonies. He was composing them regularly for his patrons, the Esterházy family, in the same way that a group of dancers in a television show make up a new dance for each week's performance. The symphony was the usual type of piece for the orchestra to play, and since there were no radios or record players 200 years ago, the only way people could hear a lot of music was 'live'.

Part of Haydn's manuscript for 'The heavens are telling', one of the choruses from The Creation

As well as symphonies and string quartets, Haydn wrote a lot of other music, for example, his cello and trumpet concertos. One of the best known of his oratorios is *The Creation*, a cheerful choral work in which Haydn uses the orchestra to create some clever dramatic effects. The composer later said that he knelt down and prayed daily in order to help him to write this work. When it was first performed in Vienna in 1798 the composer was as impressed as the audience: 'One moment I was as cold as ice; the next I was on fire. More than once I was afraid I should have a stroke.'

Questions
1 As a boy, Haydn had a good treble voice. How did it help him?
2 What happened when Haydn's voice broke?
3 How did Haydn first make a living on his own?
4 What were Haydn's first real jobs?
5 Why was Haydn fortunate in working for the Esterházy family?

The emperor Frederick the Great was also a patron of the arts. He is seen here playing the flute

6 What nick-name has Haydn been given, and why?

7 What musical form did Haydn use in his symphonies?

8 Name two popular pieces by Haydn which are *not* symphonies or string quartets.

9 Describe *The Creation* as fully as you can in your own words.

10 Describe Haydn's reaction when he first heard *The Creation*.

Things to do

1 In *The Creation*, Haydn used what is often called 'word-painting'. This means that he often emphasized the meanings of words through the music he wrote for them. For example, if the word 'low' was sung, then a low note might be used for the words; or the tune might gradually rise up if the word 'climb' had to be sung. Next time you make up some music in class, see if you can use 'word-painting' by putting some words to music in this way. Here are some examples to help you:

Climb-ing up   jump-ing   slow — ly   fall — ing   twist — ing   round. __

Here is an example of word-painting from *The Creation*, the tenor air 'Now vanish before thy holy beams'.

Allegro moderato (moderately fast)

Down __ they   sink   in the   deep   a — byss   To   end — less   night.

2 Haydn wrote more symphonies than any other well known composer. Look through this book (and any other reference book on music, such as *The Oxford Junior Companion to Music*) and try to find out how many symphonies the following composers wrote. Design a chart which will show this information:
Haydn, Mozart, Schubert, Beethoven, Mendelssohn, Brahms.

3 Just as Bach is often compared to Handel, so Haydn is often compared to Mozart. For example, together they are largely responsible for the development of the symphony and of sonata form. But how similar were their *lives*? Look through this chapter on Haydn, and the next one, on Mozart, and compare these composers' backgrounds. Then try to write about the things in their lives that were similar and the things that were different.

Mozart (1756–1791)

There are two reasons why many people think that Mozart was the greatest musician the world has ever known. First, he was a brilliant performer, and could memorize music, improvise, and perform other musical feats at a very early age; secondly, when he was older he composed some of the most popular music that has ever been written.

It is not surprising that when Mozart was a small boy he attracted a lot of attention. It was only natural that his father, Leopold, should want to show off his son to all the world, especially as this was an attractive way of making money. So Mozart's earliest years were spent travelling around Europe, performing to as many people as there were who wanted to see him.

Wolfgang Mozart had an elder sister, Maria Anna, nicknamed Nannerl, who was also talented. In 1762, when Wolfgang was only six, his father took them both to play before the Elector (Prince) of Bavaria. After another journey, this time to Vienna, the family went to London, where they stayed until the summer of 1765. Mozart was now nine years old, and for the first time he began to learn how to write music. His teacher was J. C. Bach, youngest son of the best known member of that musical family, J. S. Bach.

While they were in England Leopold Mozart fell dangerously ill, and since the children were not allowed to disturb their father by playing instruments, young Wolfgang spent all of his time composing. Under the guidance of J. C. Bach, Mozart produced his first three symphonies in London.

The Austrian composer Wolfgang Amadeus Mozart

Mozart's birthplace in Salzburg, Austria

Mozart, aged six, taking a bow after playing the piano at the court of the Empress Maria Theresa in Vienna

Between the ages of 13 and 17 Mozart went on three tours to Italy. In those days it was particularly important for all hopeful composers to have some success in at least one Italian city. While in Rome, he copied out from memory a complicated piece of church music, Allegri's *Miserere*, after hearing it only once!

Unfortunately the successes of Mozart's youth did not last. It seemed as though Mozart the 'boy-wonder' was more interesting than Mozart the young man. Many people who had been kind to him when he was a boy were now no longer interested in him as a composer.

Things went from bad to worse. While staying in Paris, Mozart's mother died, and later he discovered that the girl he had planned to marry had gone off with someone else. On returning to Salzburg he took a new job as court organist to the local Archbishop, but soon found out that it was poorly paid. He resigned, and was then promptly kicked out (literally!) by the Archbishop's assistant.

However, Mozart also had *good* fortune in his own lifetime. Some of his operas were instant successes, and he sometimes had more work than he could cope with. There were also times when he entertained some very important musicians at his house.

Strangely enough, Mozart ended up marrying the sister of the girl he had originally hoped to marry, but his new wife was not very good at running a home or looking after the little money that the family had. So although Mozart's last ten years were full of his best compositions, his domestic life was usually highly disorganized and rather uncomfortable.

Mozart's music

In spite of Mozart's fame as a young performer, his earliest compositions were relatively simple. So although he is often

The young Mozart with his father and sister Nannerl. This famous picture was probably painted when the composer was seven or eight years old

Manuscript of one of Mozart's string quartets. Mozart wrote a lot of chamber music, including over 20 string quartets

remembered as someone who began composing when very young, he should not be judged by these early pieces.

In fact, it is his last works which are thought to be his best: for example, the last of his 41 symphonies (the 'Jupiter'), which was the first symphony to make its last movement more important than its first. Symphony No. 40, in G minor, is so popular that part of it once appeared in a slightly jazzed-up form in the pop music charts.

Mozart did more than anyone else in his time to promote the clarinet. He wrote a clarinet concerto and a clarinet quintet, as well as many pieces which used what at that time was a new instrument. Other concertos were written for the bassoon, flute, and oboe. There are also the four horn concertos, of which the last movement of the fourth is perhaps the best known.

Mozart also wrote 29 piano concertos. These cover the whole of Mozart's life, from the earliest one, written in London and arranged from pieces by J. C. Bach, to the last, composed in the year that he died.

The seven most important of Mozart's operas were written in the last eleven years of his life, though he wrote another seven operas before them. They range from *The Marriage of Figaro*, a comedy, to the more serious *Don Giovanni*. Mozart's operatic output alone would have been enough to make him famous as a composer, but it is even more remarkable to think that these works were written under very poor conditions. For example, each part had to be planned around the abilities of a particular singer, who might want the part changed, and many of the opera stories were also difficult to work with.

As if this was not enough, the audience Mozart was writing for, like all 18th-century opera audiences, only half paid attention to the performance. The rest of the time was spent in eating, playing cards, or just talking!

Questions

1   Give two reasons why Mozart is often thought of as the greatest musician the world has ever known.
2   How did Mozart spend his earliest years?
3   Which composer taught Mozart composition in London?
4   Why were Mozart's Italian tours important?
5   What unusual feat did Mozart perform while in Rome?
6   How did people's attitudes to Mozart change as he got older?
7   Describe any one of the less fortunate events in Mozart's life.
8   Describe Mozart's wife in your own words. Do you think she helped Mozart?

Title page from the score of The Marriage of Figaro. *The page-boy is discovered eavesdropping by his master*

Papageno the bird-catcher, a character from another of Mozart's operas, The Magic Flute

9 Explain how Mozart helped to make one particular instrument popular.

10 How do you think Mozart's piano concertos tell us something about the composer?

Things to do

1 The opening tunes of three of Mozart's best known pieces are printed below. Some of the notes have been left out, where there is a cross above the stave. Try to fill in the missing notes yourself, while your teacher plays the tunes to you on the piano or you listen to a recording.

Eine kleine Nachtmusik
Allegro (brightly)

Strings

Symphony No.40 in G minor
Allegro molto (quite quickly)

Strings

Rondo from Horn Concerto No.4 in E♭
Allegro vivace (fast and lively)

Horn in E♭ (as sounds)

2 Mozart wrote a lot of music in his short lifetime. Look through this book to find out which other composers died young, and then design a chart which includes their names, dates and most important compositions.

3 Choose any one of the incidents in Mozart's life which are mentioned in this chapter, and write about it. You can either use your own imagination, or you can look up the details in a music reference book, such as *The Oxford Junior Companion to Music*. You could turn your writing into a short play if you liked.

Keyboard instruments

Keyboard instruments are ones which have the keys of all their notes arranged in a line. The most common keyboard instruments used today are the **piano** and **organ**.

Although the organ has existed for many hundreds of years, the piano is less than three hundred years old. Before the 18th century the only keyboard instruments, apart from the organ, were the **clavichord** and a group of instruments including the **harpsichord**. Although these earlier instruments were gradually replaced by the piano, they have been revived in this century.

An elaborate church organ built in Victorian times

The organ

This is one of the oldest of all musical instruments. Today many organs are electric, and their sound comes out of loudspeakers. But the pipe organs that you usually hear in churches work in the same way as the original instruments.

The first very simple organs were built by the Greeks and Romans, but after the collapse of the Roman Empire the instruments seem to have been forgotten until about 1100, when **portative** organs began to appear. These were small enough to carry around. Gradually organs got bigger, and were made with more than one keyboard. In the 19th and 20th centuries very large organs were made, often with four or even five keyboards.

All pipe organs produce their notes by blowing air through pipes, most of which are quite large, rather like giant tin whistles. Pipes of 16 feet are quite normal for bass notes, and some pipes are even as long as 64 feet! When the player presses a note on the keyboard this opens a **valve** on the **wind chest** and lets air into a pipe. Different kinds of sound can be produced by different shaped pipes, and the sound produced by the player will depend on what **stop** is pulled out. J. S. Bach is perhaps the best known composer of organ music.

The clavichord

This instrument was popular from the 16th to the 18th centuries, but was no longer used very much after the invention of the piano. In the 20th century, however, it has become popular again, partly perhaps because it is a simple, small and quiet keyboard instrument. It is also fairly cheap to manufacture.

The strings of a clavichord are hit by a piece of metal called a **tangent**, which remains on the string for as long as the key is pressed down. The instrument is usually shaped like an oblong box, often hardly bigger than a briefcase, which can either rest on a stand or on a table.

A lady playing the harpsichord in the 17th century

family are produced by the strings being *plucked* and not hit. Although loud and soft sounds can be made, it is difficult to make any gradual distinction between loud and soft notes. For this reason you will often find that harpsichord music has a lot of 'decorations', which prolong the sound of notes.

The sound of a harpsichord or spinet is produced by a plectrum on the end of a length of wood called a **jack**. This plucks the strings when the key is pressed down. Harpsichords often had two keyboards, and each one could produce a different sound. Bach, Handel, Couperin, Scarlatti and Rameau are amongst the most famous harpsichord composers.

The piano

In 1709 an Italian named Cristofori produced a harpsichord 'col piano e forte', which means 'with soft and loud'. In other words, unlike the harpsichord, this new instrument could go from soft to loud gradually, by playing one note louder (or softer) than another note. For the first time a keyboard instrument could respond to a player's *touch*, because the strings were hit

As it is very quiet the clavichord is unsuitable for a concert hall, but ideal for playing in an ordinary room without disturbing other people. It is not surprising that organists used the clavichord to practise on, though a lot of clavichord music was also specially written for the instrument, particularly in Germany between 1650 and 1750. Buxtehude and J. S. Bach both composed for the clavichord at this time.

Harpsichords and spinets

At about the same time that the clavichord was popular, so too were **harpsichords** and **spinets**. The harpsichord is the larger of these two instruments, and it was the most important keyboard instrument of the 16th and 17th centuries, until it was replaced by the piano. Like the clavichord, it has become popular in this century, and a certain amount of music has again been specially written for it.

Unlike the clavichord and the piano, the notes on the instrument of the harpsichord

A piano of 1819 made by the famous piano-maker John Broadwood, similar to the one supplied by the same firm to Beethoven (see page 27)

by a hammer with the same force as that used to press the key. Since this instrument could play both *piano* (soft) and *forte* (loud), it became known as the **pianoforte**, or **piano** for short.

Early piano composers were J. S. Bach's sons: C. P. E. Bach and J. C. Bach. As the instrument became more popular, however, composers such as Beethoven, Chopin and Liszt wrote more powerful and dramatic music for it. So the instruments had to be built with iron frames to withstand this increased force. (The earliest pianos would have simply collapsed if they had not been developed and strengthened!) A new mechanism to ensure greater efficiency in the production of sound was also invented. The piano's range was extended from five octaves to six by 1819. In the 19th century it was a popular instrument in the home and lots of different shapes and sizes were designed and manufactured. In the 20th century composers wrote for it as part of the orchestra.

Electronic keyboard instruments

The most popular of these is probably the **electric organ**. Sound is created not by blowing air through pipes (see **organ**, above), but by electronic signals. These are switched on and off by pressing the keys. The signals are then amplified and heard through large loudspeakers. The electric organ can imitate very many sounds, depending on how its controls are adjusted by the player.

The **electric piano** is a special kind of electric organ, designed to imitate the sound of a piano. As with the organ, the keys are really special switches to control the electric signals that make the sound. These are sometimes 'pressure sensitive', so that the harder you press the keys, the louder the sound is.

A large synthesizer in an electronic studio

The **synthesizer** is a very new kind of 'instrument', used both by 'electronic' composers and rock bands. Like the electric organ, it creates sound electronically, by using oscillators, but allows far more control over the development of the sound. For example, it can be given any rhythm pitch or tone; it can also be 'filtered' and 'shaped'. In short, the synthesizer creates any existing or new sound by putting together (*synthesizing*) all the parts that make up that sound.

Questions

1. What two sorts of organ can be heard today?
2. How do pipe organs produce their sound?
3. How are the notes of a clavichord produced?
4. Why is a clavichord unsuitable for the concert hall?
5. How do harpsichords and spinets differ from clavichords and pianos?
6. Name some well known harpsichord composers.
7. How did the piano get its full name?
8. Explain how the piano works.
9. Explain how electric organs work.
10. What is a synthesizer? How does it work?

Things to do

1   The following extracts of keyboard music have all been written for particular instruments. Can you tell which extract is for which instrument? How do you know?

Con espressione (expressively)

Field: Sonata No.4 in B

mezzo

R.H. Ch. Flute(s) 8. (4.) [or soft Gamba 8.]
L.H. Sw. soft 16.8.
Ped. coupled to Gt. Flute 4.

Adagio (slowly)

G. Merkel: Study Op. 182, No. 29

(4 ft.)

Gaily

Couperin: Les moissonneurs

2   Design a chart all about keyboard instruments, as follows, and fill in the answers:

Instrument	Family	How are notes produced?	Near relations	Any other information
Violin Piano etc . . .				

3   Imagine that you had to describe any one keyboard instrument to someone who came from a place where music hardly exists. One example might be a man in space. You would obviously have to explain everything in great detail. Write an imaginary conversation that might take place if you did this, choosing any one instrument to talk about.

Beethoven (1770–1827)

Ludwig van Beethoven was born at Bonn, a small town where the Elector (Prince) of Cologne had his palace. Beethoven's father sung in the Elector's chapel, and when he saw that young Ludwig was good at music, he tried to make the boy into a child performer, just as Mozart's father had done (see page 19). He made Ludwig practise the piano and violin a lot every night, so that by the time the boy was seven he was able to give a local concert.

Unfortunately Beethoven's father drank more than was good for him, and so he was not as well organized at promoting his son as Mozart's father had been. In any case, young Beethoven was not very bothered about pleasing people, and so for these two reasons he never became the child prodigy that his father would have liked him to be. Perhaps it was just as well that his musical training was taken over by the court organist, Neefe, who within two years taught Beethoven enough to make him his deputy. In another two years, by the time Beethoven was 14, he was the official assistant court organist.

At the age of 16 Beethoven visited Vienna, where he met Mozart (then 31) who may have given him some lessons in composition. He stayed there only a few weeks though, before returning to Bonn when his mother died. Beethoven now had to take full responsibility for the family, since his father was in no fit state to earn a proper living. So Beethoven had to try to earn more money to support his brothers, which he did by teaching and by playing the viola for the local opera.

In 1792, when he was 22, Beethoven again visited Vienna. This time he never returned, partly because his father died soon after he left, but also because Cologne was invaded by Napoleon. In Vienna Beethoven made a living out of playing and teaching the piano, and learned composition from several teachers, including Haydn (see page 16)

By the age of 25 Beethoven's first piano concerto was performed, and five years later his first symphony. During these early years he became more and more popular, yet he was also well known for his rudeness and bad behaviour, especially in the company of the aristocracy

It was soon after he was 30 that Beethoven began to realize he was going deaf. He had suspected this for some time, and now that he knew for certain he tried hard to fight against this terrible affliction. He wrote more music than usual, perhaps because he realized that he only had a few years in which to hear it.

The German composer Ludwig van Beethoven

Beethoven's study, left in total disorder after his death

Beethoven also had other problems. He was involved in a court case over whether he or his sister-in-law should look after his nephew Karl. In the end he won, but the boy proved to be more trouble than Beethoven might have thought he was worth.

Yet in spite of his personal tragedy of deafness, and his untidy personal life, Beethoven continued to rise above these things and even in his last years managed to write great music.

Beethoven's music

There are two important reasons why Beethoven's music was different from the music of Mozart and Haydn. First, Beethoven was one of the earliest composers able to write music that *he* wanted to write, rather than the pieces that some Prince or Archbishop paid him a salary to compose. So in one way Beethoven may have been able to put more effort into his symphonies and concertos, since he was not having to write them regularly.

Secondly, changing attitudes helped Beethoven a lot. The French Revolution made many people, including Beethoven, think differently about the aristocracy. Many artists and musicians also began to value their freedom. Certainly Beethoven did, and at times he was even rude to noblemen. Perhaps this attitude helped to make his music rather more adventurous than the music of earlier composers.

In the 57 years of his life Beethoven wrote many different pieces, including nine symphonies and five piano concertos, as well as popular piano pieces such as *Für Elise* and the 'Moonlight' sonata. This may not seem very much compared with the number of compositions of Haydn and Mozart, but this is because there were other important differences between these composers and Beethoven. His pieces were usually much longer and more complicated, and he also found it difficult to compose as quickly as Mozart and Haydn.

The opening theme of Beethoven's third symphony (the 'Eroica') is a good example of his longer themes.

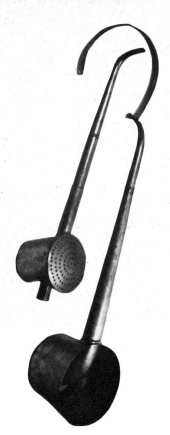

The ear trumpets Beethoven used after he became deaf

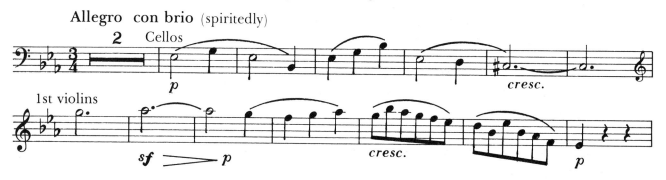

Beethoven's music includes nine symphonies, five piano concertos, an opera (*Fidelio*), two masses and a great deal of piano and chamber music. Perhaps his best known piece of music is his fifth symphony.

Questions

1 How did Beethoven's father try to copy Mozart's father?
2 Give one reason why Beethoven did not become a child prodigy.
3 Who was Beethoven's teacher at the age of ten?
4 Why did Beethoven stay in Vienna on his second visit?
5 How did Beethoven earn his living while in Vienna?
6 Explain how Beethoven behaved in front of other people.
7 What effect did Beethoven's deafness seem to have on his work?
8 Explain one aspect of Beethoven's problems in his private life.
9 Describe the conditions Beethoven lived in during the last few years of his life.
10 Why was Beethoven's music different to that of earlier composers?

Things to do

1a Next time you make up music of your own in class, try to think of how *long* your tunes are. You could either write short, fairly simple ones, as Mozart often did; or you could make them longer and more complicated, as Beethoven sometimes did.
1b Here is the opening theme of Mozart's Symphony No. 39. Look at it carefully, and compare it with that of the 'Eroica'. Write down a list of all the main differences you can find.

2 The French Revolution, which took place in 1789, had an important effect on the development of music. Make your own time chart, showing the date of the revolution and the dates of the great composers who lived just before, during and after it. Does your chart tell you anything?
3 On his first visit to Vienna Beethoven met Mozart, and would probably have liked to have had lessons from him regularly. Try to imagine the boy's impressions of Mozart, and write an imaginary letter from Beethoven to one of his friends at home which describes this meeting. It might help you to read about Mozart first (page 19).

Napoleon Bonaparte. Beethoven dedicated his Eroica Symphony to him but later crossed out the dedication when he discovered that Napoleon had declared himself Emperor

Classical and Romantic music

The words **classical** and **romantic** music have often been used in this book. Exactly what do they mean? One of the problems with the words classical music is that they are often used to mean all 'serious' music written by 'serious' composers. For example, we might call the music of all the composers in this book classical music. It is all right to use the expression classical music in this way, but it also has a more precise meaning.

The composers in this book cover a period of approximately 400 years, from the middle of the 15th century to the present day. During this time music has changed and developed a great deal: the kind of music being written by modern composers today is very different from the music that Tchaikovsky wrote in the 19th century; and the music of Mozart is just as different from the music of the Elizabethans. To make it easier to talk about the different sorts of music, we give names to different types which were written in different times in history.

Classical music is the name we give to the music of composers at the time of Haydn and Mozart. Beethoven's early music can be called classical too (though some people call him the first romantic composer) and so can Schubert's. There are also many less well known classical composers, all of whom composed in the period from about 1750–1825.

But what is classical music in this *special* sense like? If you look at the chapter on Beethoven, you'll see that one of the differences between his later music and the music of Haydn and Mozart was that Beethoven's tunes were longer or more complicated (look at page 28 and compare the length of the theme from Beethoven's 'Eroica' symphony with that of

A concert of classical music in 1799

Mozart's Symphony No 39 on page 29). So you could say that the tunes in classical music are fairly simple and short, whereas in Romantic music they tend to be longer.

This doesn't make the music any worse than other types of music; in fact, one of the reasons that many people like classical music is that they find it easy to listen to, because they often know what is going to happen next. Some people, however, prefer later styles of music, which they perhaps think of as more 'exciting'.

Romantic music is the name we usually give to the style of music which came after classical music. Beethoven has been called the first romantic composer, and although some people argue about this, many people would agree that the composers in this book from Mendelssohn to Berlioz were all romantic composers. What does this mean? It doesn't have much to do with romance as we usually think of it today, of course!

A more intimate, Romantic concert: the composer Liszt playing to a group of friends

Most of the romantic composers have tried at some time to suggest ideas, feelings or moods through their music. Some have even tried to suggest actual pictures in the listener's mind: perhaps their music has tried to tell a story. We call this kind of music **programme music**. A good example of this is Berlioz's *Fantastic Symphony*, which is about a man who falls in love with a woman, and eventually kills her. The movements of the symphony have titles, such as *Dreams*, and some of the tunes are meant to suggest actual events or people: for example, there is a tune which occurs several times throughout the symphony which represents the woman in the story.

Classical music hardly ever does anything like this, and although there is **word-painting** in some classical choral music, the composers are mainly concerned with the *structure* of their music, that is, the way in which all the different tunes are put together. Classical composers, for example, developed **sonata form** (see page 40).

So *who* are the romantic composers? One of the reasons why Beethoven is often thought to be the first has been given on page 30. His *Pastoral* symphony is another reason: this has titles for each movement, such as 'by the brook'.

Although some people argue that Beethoven's music was classical, and not romantic, few people would disagree with the following list of romantic composers:

Berlioz; Chopin; Schumann; Wagner; Verdi; Brahms; Tchaikovsky; Liszt; Mendelssohn.

Beethoven making sketches for his Pastoral Symphony. Some people think of him as the first Romantic composer

Questions

1 What is the usual meaning of the expression **classical music**?

2 What is the more precise meaning of the expression **classical music**?

3 Name three classical composers, using the precise meaning of the word.

4 Name one of the differences between the themes of Mozart and Beethoven.

5 What do we mean by **romantic music**?

6 What were romantic composers often trying to do through their music?

7 Give an example of a piece of romantic music and explain why it is a good example.

8 In just one way, *some* classical music is a little like romantic music. Explain this.

9 What particular kind of structure did classical composers develop?

10 Explain why Beethoven is sometimes thought of as a romantic composer.

Things to do

1 If you make up music in class, try to copy classical composers by using a plan, such as binary or ternary form:

Binary Form
This uses two tunes, one after the other:
tune A —— tune B

Ternary Form
In Ternary Form, there are three parts to the music, but the first and last parts are the same:
tune A —— tune B —— tune A
You could then try to do what romantic composers often did, which was to tell a story in music. First, find, or make up, a simple story (even a fairy tale will do!), and make up some short tunes to fit the important characters. Then try to put your tunes together into a complete piece.

2 Draw a chart of music and composers which covers the classical and romantic periods in music. It should include all the important composers of each period and some of their best known pieces.

3 **Baroque**, **Impressionist** and **Avant-garde** are also types of music, like **Classical** and **Romantic**. Try to find out what sort of music these words refer to, and who their main composers are, or have been. You could use a music reference book, such as *The Oxford Junior Companion to Music*, to find out, or you could look through some of the other chapters in this book. Write down everything you find out.

Schubert (1797–1828)

Franz Schubert was born in a suburb of Vienna. His father was a rather badly paid schoolteacher who played the cello. The whole family was musical, but Franz soon managed to play the violin a lot better than his brother and sister, and by the age of six he seemed to be very talented.

At first he was taught by his father and brother, and then by the organist of the local church. When he was 11 he won a scholarship to the Imperial Choir School, where he received a general and musical education. He became first violinist in the school orchestra, and sometimes deputized for the conductor.

At the early age of 13 he started to write his own music, and was so successful that a famous local teacher, Salieri (who had also taught Beethoven), agreed to give him lessons. But as the days of patronage were now over, and since Schubert was not as good a performer as Beethoven, he was not able to earn a living at music alone. So when he left the choir school at the age of 16 he went back to his father's school, this time to teach.

By now Schubert was composing a great deal in his spare time. In fact he wanted to be able to spend more time on composing and less on teaching, which he didn't really enjoy. So when Franz von Schober, a rich local young man, offered him free accommodation, Schubert accepted, and at the age of 19 he left his father's school.

A year later Schubert met Vogl, the famous singer. Vogl encouraged Schubert to write songs for him to sing, and made sure that the composer accompanied him at the performances. This was very good publicity for Schubert.

Although there seemed to be less aristocratic music-making on a grand scale in Vienna at this time, people were still very involved in music. Members of the 'middle class' would regularly hold musical evenings at each others' houses, and play and sing to each other. This was where Schubert played much of his music.

Schubert was one of the many great artists who lived for only a very short time, though this did not stop him composing a tremendous amount of music. He died of typhus at the age of 31, still comparatively poor: an auction of all his property after his death fetched about £2.50.

The Austrian composer Franz Schubert

Musical evenings were popular in Vienna. This painting shows Schubert playing for friends, including the singer Vogl

Schubert's music

Some composers seem to struggle very hard to write their music. The tunes do not come very easily to them, and they spend a lot of time revising them before their compositions are complete. A few, however, just write down what seems to come 'flowing' out of their heads. Mozart was this sort of composer, and so was Schubert. Although Schubert certainly did revise some of his music, he composed at such a terrific rate that any other composer would have considered him abnormal!

In his short lifetime Schubert wrote over 600 songs and nine symphonies (if Beethoven had died as young as Schubert did, he would have only written one symphony, not nine). In just one year Schubert wrote 140 songs, 30 in just one month and 15 in two days! He wrote so much music, so fast, that he has been compared to Mozart as a genius.

Schubert is perhaps best known for his songs. No other composer before him had concentrated on song writing, so one of Schubert's achievements is in making the song a standard and important musical form. Obviously he studied and worked on the *way* songs were written too, and made them much more important than an ordinary tune with a background accompaniment. Some of his songs were simple, but others were dramatic and often long. His accompaniments were very important too, often just as important as the vocal part. 'The Erl King', 'The Trout' and 'The Wanderer' are among Schubert's best known songs.

Schubert continued to use **classical** form in his instrumental music (for example, **sonata form** in the first movements of symphonies and sonatas—see page 40). But in some ways he was like the later romantic composers in the importance he gave to melody, and in his virtuoso writing for the piano. (Schubert admitted that even he could not play his Wanderer fantasy himself.) His short pieces, such as the *Impromptus* and *Moments Musicaux*, were also the kind of piece without any strict form which was later to be written by romantic composers.

Schubert in a café in Vienna

An illustration from Schubert's famous song The Erl King

Questions

1 Who were Schubert's first teachers?
2 What two positions did Schubert hold in his school orchestra?
3 Give two reasons why Schubert could not earn a living at music alone.
4 Who helped Schubert to leave his father's school, and how?

Schubert and his friends on an outing. Schubert, wearing spectacles, is at the back of the carriage

Schubert enjoyed a joke and wrote this piece using cats instead of notes

5 What friendship helped Schubert's music to reach a wider audience?

6 In what way did Schubert compose?

7 Which other composer could you compare with Schubert, and why?

8 How did Schubert develop the song?

9 In what ways did Schubert foreshadow the later romantic composers?

10 In what way did Schubert copy the classical composers?

Things to do

Q. 1a and 1b—see next page

2 You have read that Schubert composed a lot of music in his short life. Make a chart of the following composers, showing the lengths of their lives and the approximate number of important compositions they wrote (symphonies, concertos, operas, oratorios, etc.): Mozart, Schubert, Bach, Handel, Haydn, Chopin. You will need to look though this book to do this.

3 Schubert is famous for the songs he composed. Which other composers have specialized in songs or other kinds of vocal music (operas, oratorios, etc.)? Look through this book, and any other music reference books, such as *The Oxford Junior Companion to Music*, to find out. Write a short paragraph on the vocal music of each composer you find.

1a   Next time you play your own music in class, try to make up a song. You could use 'word-painting' (see page 18) to help.

1b   Here is an extract from one of Schubert's songs, 'Frozen Tears' from *The Winter's Journey*:

Non troppo lento (not too slowly)

Write down all the things you notice about it, however unimportant they may seem. Here are some questions to help you:

i   What things in the music suggest that this is a sad song?

ii   In which bars of the accompaniment do you think the composer was trying to create the idea of tears *falling*? Explain your answer.

Mendelssohn (1809–1847)

Unlike many of the composers in this book, Felix Mendelssohn came from a very comfortable background. His father was a rich banker in Berlin, and so Felix was able to have everything that he wanted when he was a child, including the best music teachers that money could buy. His family enjoyed music, and encouraged Felix to be involved in it. In fact they encouraged him in anything which was artistic.

His mother gave him piano lessons at first, but he soon learned the piano, violin and composition with some very good teachers. He got on so well with the piano that he gave a public concert at the age of eight, and one of his choral compositions was performed at another public concert when he was only ten. By the time he was 15 he had written his first symphony, and at the age of 17 he wrote one of his most famous pieces of music, the *Midsummer Night's Dream* overture.

The German composer Felix Mendelssohn

One of the advantages of coming from a rich background was that Mendelssohn could travel wherever he liked. It was usual for rich young men to make a 'grand tour' of Europe, and when he was 20 this is what the composer did. He went to Italy, where he wrote his 'Italian' symphony, and Paris, where he met Chopin and Liszt.

Mendelssohn also paid many visits to Britain during his lifetime, and was inspired to write music about Scotland: a 'Scotch' symphony and sonata, and the *Fingal's Cave* overture. In England he was even popular with the royal family, and was on friendly terms with Queen Victoria and Prince Albert, with whom he used to play music at Buckingham Palace.

Mendelssohn was fortunate in holding a number of professional musical appointments. At the age of 23 he became conductor of the lower Rhine Festival, and then became general musical director of Dusseldorf. Two years later he was appointed conductor of the famous *Gewandhaus* orchestra at Leipzig, and eventually, after some time spent unhappily in the service of the King of Prussia, Mendelssohn became the first director of the Leipzig Conservatory of Music.

Although Mendelssohn is best known for his own musical compositions, he spent a lot of time and energy in making the music of other composers popular. It is difficult to imagine that the music of Bach, Handel, Mozart and Beethoven was not always well known or liked in the 19th century, but it is partly because of Mendelssohn that a lot of music which we know today is played. For example, when Mendelssohn was young, nobody living at that time had heard Bach's

St Matthew Passion, as it had not been performed since Bach died nearly a century earlier. Mendelssohn was given a handwritten copy of the work (which had never been published), and in 1829 he managed to get it performed. Since then it has been one of the most popular of all choral works, and is now regularly performed all over the world.

Mendelssohn died at the early age of 38, probably from overwork and nervous exhaustion.

Mendelssohn's music

A lot of Mendelssohn's music is in a happy mood, and written for enjoyment, which is why he was a very popular composer in his lifetime, especially in England. But Mendelssohn has also been criticized because his music does not always seem to be very serious, or because it lacks the special characteristics of music written by other composers.

One of the reasons for this may be that since Mendelssohn himself never had to face any great problems or struggles in order to survive, as many other composers did, so his music never reflected any difficulties. Music can often be a reflection of its composer's character: Mendelssohn's music is often carefree and polite, like the composer himself.

One interesting example of the way in which Mendelssohn's music is different from the classical music of the 18th century is the opening of his popular violin concerto. It starts with the soloist playing almost immediately, unlike the classical concertos of Mozart, which usually had a longer opening section where only the orchestra played. The middle movement of the violin concerto is also typically romantic, with its sad song-like tune.

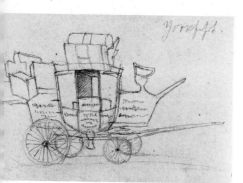

Mendelssohn liked sketching and drew this picture of the coach in which he travelled to Scotland

Andante (at a walking pace)

Mendelssohn's music includes two oratorios, four symphonies and several overtures.

Questions

1 What sort of family did Mendelssohn come from?
2 Describe any one of Mendelssohn's earliest musical experiences.
3 What unusual opportunity did Mendelssohn have at the age of 20?

4 What were the musical results of Mendelssohn's travels to Britain?

5 What was Mendelssohn responsible for doing in the world of music, apart from writing his own music?

6 Which piece of music, now famous, did Mendelssohn 'discover'?

7 How could you describe Mendelssohn's music?

8 What reasons could you give for Mendelssohn's music being the way it is (Q.7)?

9 What things make Mendelssohn's violin concerto 'romantic'?

10 How does the opening of many 'classical' concertos compare to Mendelssohn's violin concerto?

Things to do

1 Mendelssohn's visits to other countries inspired him to write music which in some way was connected with those places. Next time you make up some music of your own in class, choose one particular country, and try to connect it with your music. You could choose some of the country's well known tunes to start with, and develop your piece from them or simply join the tunes together. Here is a list of tunes from different countries to help you start:

England	*Wales*	*Scotland*
Greensleeves	Men of Harlech	Auld Lang Syne
British Grenadiers	Ash Grove	Annie Laurie
Jerusalem	All through the	Loch Lomond
Land of Hope and	Night	
Glory		

France	*U.S.A.*
Frère Jacques	John Brown's Body
La Marseillaise	Old Folks at Home

2 This chapter tells you that Mendelssohn re-discovered the music of several composers who lived before he did. Design your own time chart to show when Mendelssohn lived, as well as the composers he helped to make popular. You will need to look through this book to find the dates of the composers concerned.

3 In this chapter you can find out some of the different places that Mendelssohn went to, and some of the people he met. Choose any one particular occasion when he visited a person or a place, and *either* write an entry in a diary about it, as if you were the composer, *or* describe what you imagine might have taken place. You may find it helpful to use other music reference books to do this.

Mendelssohn was a great favourite with Queen Victoria and Prince Albert

Sonatas and Symphonies

Between them, Haydn, Mozart and Beethoven wrote a great many **sonatas** and **symphonies**. But what exactly is a sonata or a symphony? They are both pieces of music in three or four movements: a sonata is usually for one solo instrument, and a symphony is for an orchestra. Both these types of composition developed from the **suite**, which was a popular form of music in the time of Purcell, Bach and Handel.

A sonata or symphony is like a suite, as it consists of three or four shorter pieces (**movements**) connected together to make one long one. Each movement is arranged to contrast with the ones next to it, perhaps by being a different speed.

Beethoven, whose ninth symphony includes parts for solo singers and chorus

Haydn, the 'Father of Symphony'

Mozart, who wrote over 40 symphonies

The first movement
This is usually the longest and most important in a classical sonata or symphony. Often it is in a particular kind of form which we call **sonata form**, and is made up in the following way.

First the composer takes a tune that he has invented (called the **first subject**), and then he takes another (the **second subject**) in a different key. Between these two tunes he usually puts a short section leading from the one to the other, called a **bridge passage**.

After the second subject the composer usually adds on an extra bit which we call the **coda**. The whole of this first section is called the **exposition**, because it *exposes* the main tunes and musical ideas which make up the movement. Often the composer tells the performer to repeat this exposition before going on, in order to get the tunes firmly fixed in the listener's mind.

The next section is called the **development**, quite simply because the tunes and ideas we have heard in the exposition are developed, which means they are changed and added to. Here the composer uses parts of either of the tunes and changes key several times as well. But there are no special rules for the development, and so almost anything might happen in this part of the movement.

Lastly there is the **recapitulation**, where the tunes first heard in the exposition are now repeated, though both subjects are usually in the same key here. There is often a longer coda this time to round off the whole movement.

A diagram of the first movement, in sonata form, might look like this:

Dancing the minuet

EXPOSITION				
Introduction	1st subject	Bridge passage	2nd subject	Coda

DEVELOPMENT

RECAPITULATION			
1st subject	Bridge passage	2nd subject	Coda

The other movements

The middle movement of a sonata or symphony is usually slow and expressive, but if there are four movements then the second of the two middle movements will often be a **minuet** and **trio**, or a **scherzo**. A minuet is a stately but graceful dance-like piece in 3/4 time. The trio is simply another minuet which contrasts with the first. The minuet and trio are arranged like this in the movement:

MINUET . . . TRIO . . . MINUET

Scherzo means a joke, and so this type of movement is usually very lively.

The last movement of a sonata or symphony is frequently in sonata form, like the first movement. But sometimes other forms are used, such as the **rondo**. This has a main subject (**A**) that keeps being repeated in between different tunes:

A B A_2 C A_3 D A_4 . . .

Trying to understand music just by reading about it is not always easy. The best way to experience 'classical' musical form is to hear it, by playing or listening to plenty of sonatas and symphonies, especially by such composers as Haydn and Mozart.

Questions

1   How are a sonata and symphony alike?
2   What is the connection between a suite and a sonata?
3   What do we call the pieces or parts which make up a sonata or symphony?
4   How many parts are there usually to a sonata or symphony?
5   In a three-movement sonata or symphony, how might the middle movement contrast with the first and last ones?
6   How many main tunes (**subjects**) are there in the first movement of a sonata written in **sonata form**?
7   In sonata form, what are the names for: (a) the short section which rounds off the end of the exposition? (b) the short part which connects the two subjects in an exposition?
8   What is the name of the dance-like piece often found in a sonata or symphony?
9   What is the name for the humorous movement often found in a four-movement sonata or symphony?
10 Describe a **rondo**.

Things to do

1a Next time you make up some music of your own in class, see if you can put together some tunes in **rondo form**. Here is a simple plan for you to follow:

tune A —— tune B —— tune A —— tune C —— tune A

1b Listen to the last movement of Mozart's fourth horn concerto and try to draw your own rondo diagram, like the one in this chapter, to show exactly what is happening. Here are three different tunes you will hear:

A   Allegro vivace (fast and lively)
Horn in E♭ (sounds 6th lower)

B

C

2   Copy out and colour the diagram of sonata form on a large piece of paper to make your own classroom poster. You could even decorate it by adding the parts of actual music that have come from a sonata or symphony.

3   Read the first part of this chapter, which tells you about sonata form. Then write out a chart which explains sonata form, starting like this:

Introduction	This is sometimes included to introduce the first subject etc . . .
1st subject etc . . .	

The orchestra

So far in this book you may have read about several composers who regularly wrote music for the orchestra. Haydn and Mozart, for example, wrote a total of 150 symphonies. Although composers before the time of Haydn and Mozart also wrote orchestral music, the orchestra began to be used more and more from their time onwards. It grew larger and larger as composers wrote parts for extra instruments, till eventually it became the large symphony orchestra we know today.

We often think of the orchestra in groups (often called **families**) of instruments. The four main groups are **strings**, **woodwind**, **brass** and **percussion**.

An orchestra playing in a London park in the 1890s

An orchestra of the 17th century with very few players. Notice the conductor beating time with a roll of paper

A modern symphony orchestra: the BBC Symphony Orchestra conducted by Sir Colin Davis

Strings

These instruments include the violins, violas, cellos (their full name is **violoncello**) and double basses. There are usually several first and second violins, and then gradually less of the other instruments, with only a few basses. (In Mozart's time there were sometimes only one or two used.)

All these instruments work in the same way, and although they are different in size, they are so alike in every other way that you might think they really are like a family, with 'baby' violins and 'adult' cellos and basses!

A string quartet: the instruments (left to right) are two violins, a cello and a viola

Woodwind

This family consists of the flute, and instruments with a reed which are blown: clarinets, oboes and bassoons. There are usually at least two of each of these in the orchestra. These instruments have 'near relations', such as the double bassoon, the bass clarinet, the cor anglais (like an oboe, but with a curved reed and a lower and mellower tone) and the piccolo (a small flute).

A concert in Haydn's time with the flute player taking the solo part

In the classical orchestra of Haydn and Mozart, oboes, flutes and bassoons were used a lot, but their 'near relations' were developed rather later. The clarinet appeared later still, at the beginning of the 18th century, but was not used much until Mozart realized what its possibilities were, and wrote his clarinet quintet and concerto.

Brass

These instruments date back to beyond the Middle Ages. They are played, even today, by blowing a 'raspberry' into a metal mouthpiece. Since this can be done to any simple tube (try it with a hose-pipe!), we can imagine how effective the sound of an animal horn being blown must have been in pre-historic times. This animal horn was really the first 'brass' instrument.

Today the brass family of the orchestra consists mainly of trumpets, French horns and trombones. There are also other brass instruments which are not often found in the orchestra, but are part of a brass band, such as the tuba, euphonium and cornet.

All these instruments now use a system of

A wind band of 1616 made up of the ancestors of our brass and woodwind instruments. You can see a cornett (third from the left), three shawms (early oboes), a bassoon and a trombone

valves and tubing to achieve their different notes, except the trombone, which has a slide. On any brass instrument the player can play several notes (called **harmonics**) just by altering the shape of his lips. By making the tube longer, either by using valves or a slide, the whole range of notes can be played.

Bach and Handel wrote orchestral music with parts for the first kind of trumpet, and the orchestra of Haydn and Mozart used horns, as well as the new trumpet with keys and valves. Haydn wrote a concerto for this instrument soon after it was invented, and Mozart wrote four well known horn concertos. Trombones were not used much until Beethoven's time, but from then on the brass section of the orchestra became more and more important.

Percussion

The main percussion instruments in the orchestra are the **timpani** (often called the **kettledrums**). They were originally military instruments, played by soldiers on horseback,

and were borrowed by orchestras in the time of Bach and Handel. These drums are tuned, unlike other drums in the percussion family, and so orchestras use two or three instruments, each tuned to a different note.

Until Beethoven's time these drums were usually only played in the loud parts of a piece, often when the trumpets were playing. But Beethoven encouraged their use in soft passages too, by instructing the timpanist to play rapid beats softly. In this way the instrument could play a continuous soft note, which was very effective. Gradually the timpani were used more and more, until today there are often several instruments in an orchestra and sometimes more than one player for them.

There are two other main types of orchestral

The kettledrum was a military instrument as this 16th-century woodcut shows

percussion: the **unpitched** sort (this means instruments which do not play any particular note), such as other drums, cymbals and triangles; and **pitched** percussion, such as glockenspiels, xylophones and so on. These other instruments have not been used in orchestras very much until more recent times.

Questions

1 Which stringed instruments are there most of in the orchestra?

2 What are the 'near relations' of the flute, oboe and bassoon?

3 Which one of the following composers did *not* use the clarinet, and why: Bach; Mozart; Beethoven?

4 What has never changed about brass instruments?

5 How are the different **harmonics** played on a brass instrument?

6 What makes the timpani different from other drums?

7 Explain how Beethoven used the timpani in a different way from Haydn or Mozart.

8 Which of the following percussion instruments are **unpitched**: timpani; triangle; cymbal; xylophone?

9 Which of the following are **pitched** percussion instruments: glockenspiel; tambourine; bass drum; tubular bells?

10 Which percussion instruments did Haydn and Mozart not usually use in their orchestras?

Things to do

1 If you have ever listened to Britten's *Young Person's Guide to the Orchestra*, you'll know that this is a piece of music which was specially written to explain what orchestral instruments are and how they sound. If you have your own class 'orchestra' of a few instruments (ordinary classroom percussion instruments will be suitable), try to make up your own piece based on the same idea. It won't be as complicated, of course, but you can still make up short tunes to show what the instruments can do, and perhaps even write your own script to go with them.

2 Make a poster for your classroom wall which shows four 'families' of the orchestra and their main instruments. Include any important information on your chart, and if you have any copies of instrumental music, copy out short extracts and add these too.

3 Choose any one orchestral instrument, and imagine that you have to describe it to someone who has never seen it before, such as someone from outer space. Write down the sort of conversation you might have.

Berlioz (1803–1869)

The French composer Hector Berlioz

Hector Berlioz, like Mendelssohn, was born into a prosperous family. His father was a local doctor in La Côte-Saint-André, near Grenoble in France, and he wanted Hector to become a doctor too. But Berlioz had different ideas, especially when he saw some of the unpleasant things that doctors had to do. So he decided to leave the Paris medical school in order to make a career of music, rather than medicine. As a result his father gave him only a very small amount of money to live on. But Berlioz decided to go on with his musical career in spite of his father, and an elderly composer named Le Sueur agreed to teach him.

When Berlioz was 22 he went in for an important competition called the *Prix de Rome*, which entitled the winner to study composition in Rome for three years. Although he didn't win, he wasn't put off composition, and later he entered the Paris Conservatoire of Music. He also earned some money by singing in a theatre chorus in his spare time. Berlioz went in for the *Prix de Rome* twice again, and again failed each time. However, at the age of 26 he finally won the competition with a cantata called *Sardanapalus*. It was in the same year, 1830, that he composed his *Fantastic Symphony*.

Two years later Berlioz married Harriet Smithson, the actress who had inspired him to write the *Fantastic Symphony*. But in a few years he began to regret his marriage, and finally in 1842 the couple were divorced. He now began to travel round Europe, hoping to achieve the success that he had never really had in Paris. He visited Germany first, where he met other composers, including Mendelssohn, and three years later he went to Austria and Hungary. In another two years he visited Russia, and in 1847 he went to London, where he conducted a concert of his own music. He returned to Paris in 1848, and continued writing about music in magazines.

Berlioz made visits to other countries during the next ten years. He was forced to stop composing in his 60s, however, because of illness, and died in Paris in March 1869.

Berlioz's music

One thing that is often said about Berlioz's music is that it is *different*. This is because he was very good at orchestration (writing music for the orchestra). He always thought of how each instrument would sound when he wrote its part, and so the result was very effective.

Harriet Smithson, who inspired Berlioz to write the Fantastic Symphony

A painting of Berlioz conducting his Requiem, which uses a lot of brass instruments

One of the reasons that Berlioz was able to do this may have been that he was not a good pianist. As a boy he had learnt the flute and guitar, rather than the piano, and so he didn't do what many composers do: write his music at the piano first, and then **arrange** it for an orchestra. Berlioz really wrote *for* the orchestra right from the beginning, and this is probably why his orchestral music sounds so original.

Whatever we may think of his orchestration, there is little doubt that Berlioz's music is romantic. Perhaps the best example is his *Fantastic Symphony*, which was based on his love for Harriet Smithson, a young Irish actress whom he saw in Paris when he was 23. Each movement of the symphony has titles, just like Beethoven's Pastoral Symphony (see page 31), and the piece has a **fixed idea** (*idée fixe*), which is a short line of music that represents Harriet herself. We hear this bit of music in different forms throughout the symphony.

There are two more examples which show that Berlioz was a romantic composer. First, he would not write a **concerto** (which is really a classical type of composition) even for his friend Paganini, the famous violinist. Instead, he wrote a kind of symphony, *Harold in Italy*, which had a very important part in it for the viola. (This work wasn't the only one that was connected with Italy, where Berlioz had spent three years after winning the *Prix de Rome* composers' competition. Others included his first opera, *Benvenuto Cellini*, and the *Roman Carnival* overture.)

Secondly, many of Berlioz's compositions were large and long. His *Requiem*, for example, is for a choir, soloist, brass bands, and an orchestra including a great many more brass instruments than usual. His opera, *The Trojans*, is so massive, that each of its two parts can take up a whole evening's performance!

In the fourth movement of the Fantastic Symphony *the composer imagines he has killed his beloved and is riding to his death at the guillotine*

Questions

1 What sort of background did Berlioz come from?
2 In what way did Berlioz and his father disagree about Berlioz's career?
3 What was the *Prix de Rome*?
4 Name any two of the countries which Berlioz visited, and describe anything that happened to him there.
5 Explain the connection between Berlioz's wife and a symphony he wrote.
6 Suggest one reason why Berlioz was so good at writing music for the orchestra.

7 Give an example of a romantic piece of music by Berlioz, and explain why it is romantic.

8 How did Berlioz manage to write a concerto, without *calling* it a concerto? Explain carefully in your own words.

9 Explain what other characteristics of Berlioz's music tell us he was a romantic composer.

10 Name two of Berlioz's larger compositions.

Things to do

1 Here is the **idée fixe** of Berlioz's *Fantastic Symphony*, which is meant to represent his girlfriend, Harriet Smithson:

Allegro agitato e appassionato assai (lively, agitated and rather passionate)

EITHER (a) try to use this tune in a piece of your own classroom music; OR (b) compose a piece which includes your own *idée fixe*. The *idée fixe* can be played on just one instrument, or more than one. You may find it easiest to make up a story before writing your music.

2 Design a ticket or poster for the concert which Berlioz gave in London in 1847, as you think it might have looked at that time.

3 We know that Berlioz's father didn't want his son to become a composer, and that he even went as far as to give him hardly any money to live on. Imagine the arguments that Berlioz and his father must have had about this subject, and how other members of the family may have been involved in these quarrels. EITHER (a) write some entries in a diary, as Berlioz or his father might have written them, during the time they were quarrelling; OR (b) write a short scene of one of the arguments.

Chopin (1810–1849)

The Polish composer Frédéric Chopin

Most people probably think of Chopin as a famous Polish composer, but in fact he was only *half* Polish, since his father was French. Chopin learned the piano from the age of six, and only two years later played a piano concerto at a public concert. But his father did not show off his son's great talent, as other composers' fathers had done. Instead, he made sure that Chopin had a good general education and a happy childhood.

By the time Chopin was 13, however, he was a brilliant pianist, and was already studying composition and improvisation. In those days it was important that all pianists were able to **improvise** (make up) pieces of music on their own. When Chopin was 16 he began a three year music course at the Warsaw College of Music, where one of his teachers was the director. By this time he had already had his first piece of piano music published.

Chopin had always been interested in the Polish music which was all around him, and now he was beginning to compose piano pieces which showed the influence of this music. He soon began to gain a wider musical experience by visiting other countries, such as Germany and Austria, and by meeting other musicians and composers, such as Paganini, the famous violinist.

When Chopin was 20 he left Poland for ever. After some more travelling he settled down in Paris, which was to be his home for the rest of his life. There he got to know Liszt, and later Berlioz, and became admired by more musicians. By this time he had already written two piano concertos, twelve **studies** and nine **nocturnes**, as well as several other pieces. He quickly became known in the best circles, and made his living mainly from teaching the piano to rich ladies and young girls. He preferred this to the hectic life of a travelling concert pianist.

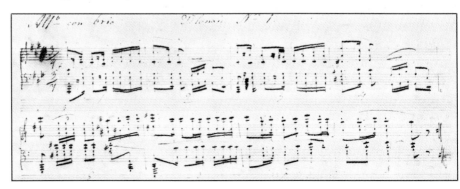

Manuscript of the opening of one of Chopin's polonaises

In 1837, when he was 27, Chopin met the unusual *female* writer, George Sand, who wore trousers and smoked cigars. From then until only two years before his death she mothered him, and looked after his rather frail health. But she was rather a bossy woman, and the two often quarrelled. They parted company in 1847, and only two years later Chopin died, aged 39, a poor and exhausted composer.

Chopin's music

Many people think of Chopin as a **romantic** composer, perhaps simply because he lived during what is known as the romantic period of musical history. In some ways, however, his music is different from the music of other composers who lived at the same time as he did.

For example, Chopin wrote what is called **absolute** music. This means that his pieces are not intended to tell a story, unlike a lot of romantic music. Secondly, he did not usually write very long pieces, or pieces for large orchestras, which was another thing these other composers often did.

However, there were some ways in which Chopin *did* follow the ideas of the composers who were alive at the time he was composing. For example, the pieces he wrote often had special titles, such as **Nocturne** or **Ballade**, and like his two piano concertos they often did not follow classical (e.g. **sonata**) form.

Perhaps the most important thing about Chopin's music was that it was written for the piano. At the time that Chopin was composing, this instrument was becoming more and more fashionable, and there were a number of very able pianists (usually called **virtuosi**) who wrote their own music, mainly in order to demonstrate their ability. Probably the best known of these virtuosi was Franz Liszt (see pages 31 and 72).

Chopin's music was greatly influenced by his Polish origins, in spite of the fact that the composer left Poland when he was 20, and never returned again. The rather sad sounding minor tones of Polish folk music can often be heard in his compositions, as well as the rhythms of Polish dances, such as the **mazurka** and **polonaise**. In fact, so great was the influence of Poland on Chopin that he can be consider the first real **nationalist** composer (see page 72).

Questions
1   What nationality was Chopin? Explain your answer.
2   Explain how Chopin's musical childhood differed from that of some other famous composers.

Chopin's friend George Sand, dressed as a man

Chopin giving a piano recital at a nobleman's house in Paris.

3 What is improvisation?

4 Where did Chopin settle down after leaving Poland?

5 What music had Chopin already written by the time he was 20?

6 Which important musicians did Chopin meet while he was in Paris?

7 Explain how Chopin earned his living in Paris.

8 What features of romantic music are *not* usually found in Chopin's music?

9 In what ways *is* Chopin's music romantic?

10 Why could Chopin be described as a **nationalist** composer?

Things to do

1 Here is an extract of a mazurka, by Chopin, in which bar lines have been missed out. Copy out the music on to manuscript paper and put the bar lines in. The left hand part will help you most. (Remember that the triplets in the right hand part only count as one crotchet altogether.)

Allegretto (not too fast)

2 Complete the chart below about the following romantic composers: Chopin, Berlioz, Schumann, Wagner, Verdi, Brahms, Tchaikovsky and Mendelssohn. Use the chapters in this book to find your information.

Name	Mainly wrote for	Some well known pieces	Wrote programme or absolute music
Chopin	The piano	Nocturnes, preludes and studies	Absolute
etc . . .			

3 Write approximately 100 of *your own* words about Chopin's life and music, just as if you were writing a programme note for a concert. Use the information in this chapter, but do not simply copy from the book. Try to find out the *most important* facts, and then write them in your own way.

Schumann (1810–1856)

The German composer Robert Schumann

Robert Schumann was born in the Saxony town of Zwickau, in 1810. His father was a bookseller and part-time publisher, and so Robert was brought up among books and music. It is not surprising that as a child he read a great deal, probably including books about past composers.

Schumann learnt the piano at the age of eight, and by the time he was in his early teens he could play anything in his father's shop. At the same time he was already composing music, writing prose and reading many of his father's own books.

When Schumann was 16 his sister killed herself. This was obviously a terrible shock for his family, and made Schumann's father's illness so much worse that he too died soon after this happened. These incidents have led some people to suggest that there may have been a streak of madness running through the Schumann family.

In 1828 Schumann went to Leipzig University to study law, partly to please his mother. There he spent a lot of time involved in books and music, and came into contact with several writers and musicians. He also began to learn the piano again, this time with Friedrich Wieck, whose nine-year-old daughter, Clara, was already a very good pianist. Schumann changed universities a year later, but still found it difficult to concentrate on law.

By the time Schumann was 20 his mother finally agreed to let him try to become a concert pianist. He had more lessons with Wieck, a teacher who seemed more interested in teaching his own daughter, Clara. In the same year Schumann had his first composition published, and in 1831 he began composition lessons.

When Schumann was 22 he invented a special mechanism to strengthen his right hand for piano technique, but tragically this crippled him for ever, and made him useless for advanced solo playing. Schumann was not put off composition though, in spite of his injury. He also spent a lot of time writing for a new music magazine which he had founded.

At the age of 25, Schumann fell in love with Clara Wieck, the 17-year-old daughter of his former piano teacher. Friedrich Wieck was against any marriage, and five years later even tried to prove in the courts that Schumann was a drunkard, and was therefore unfit to marry Clara. Friedrich lost the case, and the two were married that year.

Unlike the marriages of some composers you can read about in this

Schumann with his wife Clara, who helped make his music known all over Europe

book, this man and wife seem to have been well matched, at least musically. She was able to play anything he wrote on the piano, and in fact it was partly through her playing that his music became known all over Europe. Without her to advertise his piano compositions, perhaps Schumann would not have been as well known as he is today. However, she doesn't seem to have fully realized his mental weaknesses, and so was not really able to give him the support he needed later in life.

Soon after Schumann's marriage to Clara, he began composing pieces other than piano works, including his first symphony in 1841. After some nervous illness and a move to Dresden he even tried writing an opera. However, apart from the piano concerto, none of these pieces ever had real success, partly because Schumann did not seem able to write music very well for orchestral instruments. He always seemed to write music as if it were going to be played by a piano.

By the time Schumann was 40 he accepted the post of music director at Dusseldorf, where his main work was conducting. Unfortunately this was something that he was not at all good at, but instead of giving up quickly, he was persuaded by Clara to stay on. Three years later he gave up the post, and soon after this he had a more serious nervous illness. He died in a lunatic asylum three years later.

Schumann's music

Perhaps it is not really surprising that Schumann should be thought of as a romantic composer. Growing up in his father's shop brought him into contact with the greatest romantic writers, including Hoffmann, Goethe and Byron. In his 20s he also met several other romantic composers, such as Chopin and Mendelssohn, whom he greatly admired.

Although Schumann is often thought of as a composer for the piano (between the ages of 20 and 30 he *only* wrote piano music), he also composed an opera, choral music, four symphonies, a cello concerto and more than 250 songs, as well as two well known song-cycles. His best known piano music includes the piano concerto, *Papillons* and the *Scenes of Childhood*.

The cover of one of Schumann's collections of piano pieces for children

Questions

1 Why did Schumann read a lot as a child?
2 What tragedy occurred in the Schumann family when the composer was in his teens?
3 How did Schumann spend much of his time at university?
4 How did Schumann's studies change when he was 20?
5 What unusual tragedy occurred when Schumann was 22?
6 Whom did Schumann fall in love with when he was 25?
7 Explain how someone stood in the way of Schumann's marriage.
8 What was Schumann's final job, and why was it a disaster for him?
9 Give one reason why it is not surprising that Schumann is often considered a romantic composer.
10 Explain what is unusual about the pieces Schumann wrote between the ages of 20 and 30.

Things to do

1 Schumann's first published piece of music was based on the notes A, B, E and G. This was because he had some friends whose family name was Abeg. Try to write a very simple piece of music, or just a melody, based on the name of someone you know. If their name contains letters other than the letter names of notes, just count up beyond G, until you get to the other letter:

(*Note* The letter names of the notes above G are not, of course, their *real* letter names.)

2 Imagine the court scene when Friedrich Wieck tried to prove that Schumann was a drunkard, so that he could be prevented from marrying Clara. EITHER write a script for this scene; OR write a short newspaper report of the incident.

3 Why do you think that Schumann's mother finally allowed him to train to be a concert pianist when he was 20? What did he do or say to persuade her? Write two imaginary letters which might have passed between them. In the first, let Schumann describe his work at the university, and explain how involved he is in music. In the second his mother should explain how she feels about his taking up music as a career.

Brahms (1833–1897)

The German composer Johannes Brahms

Johannes Brahms was born in 1833 in the slums of Hamburg. His father was a badly paid double bass player, and was only able to work in the local theatre in the winter. During the summer he had to rely upon occasional work, often with a dance band.

It was not surprising that in this poor but musical environment Brahms began to show some ability in music when he was still very young. When he was eight his father arranged for him to have piano lessons. In two years Brahms had learnt so quickly that his teacher suggested the boy had lessons from a well known teacher, Eduard Marxsen, who was also a composer. Marxson taught Brahms the piano and a little composition too.

Because Brahms's family was poor, Johannes, like other children of poor families, was expected to earn some money as soon as possible, instead of staying at school. He did this by playing the piano in public houses and dance halls, and it was perhaps here that he picked up his rather rough manners which stayed with him all his life.

When he was 15, Brahms was invited to spend the summer in the country house of a music lover, and a year later he gave public concerts in Hamburg. He now began to compose seriously, and when he was 20 went on tour as the accompanist to an Hungarian violinist named Reményi. He was perhaps the influence behind the Hungarian Dances and Gypsy songs which Brahms wrote. Reményi also introduced Brahms to the young violinist Joachim, who was soon to become a close friend. Joachim already had a job at Hanover, where he arranged for Brahms and Reményi to play. He also introduced Brahms to several leading composers, such as Liszt and Wagner, as well as Schumann, with whom Brahms became friendly.

For the next few years Brahms toured locally as a pianist, taught and continued to compose. After a short time as conductor of the Philharmonic Concerts in Hamburg, he settled in Vienna at the age of thirty and remained there for the rest of his life.

Brahms's music

Although Brahms is thought of as a **romantic** composer (he lived right in the middle of the romantic period) in some ways he could almost be called a **classical** composer. He certainly approved of certain features of classical music, such as the kind of development of themes which is found in sonata form. He also disliked many of the

Brahms's friend, the violinist Joachim

Manuscript of one of Brahms's piano pieces, the Rhapsody in E flat

features of romantic music, such as the programme music (see page 31) of Berlioz and Liszt. Most of all he disliked the new 'experimental' music of Wagner.

Some of Brahms's ideas about music may have resulted from the rather strict composition lessons which he had with Eduard Marxsen. Marxsen introduced Brahms to the work of Bach and Beethoven, which was to influence the composer in later life. So Brahms was a composer who managed to keep his romantic instinct under control, and allowed the composers of the past, especially the great German ones, to influence his music.

Some of Brahms's best known music was composed when he was quite old. In fact some other composers didn't even reach the age at which Brahms wrote his first symphony (43), which one conductor rudely called 'Beethoven's 10th symphony' (to show how much influence Beethoven had over Brahms). Brahms's fourth symphony, probably his most popular, was composed when he was over 50, while the difficult second piano concerto was written at the age of 48. The popular *Academic Festival Overture* was composed only a year before that.

Brahms didn't *just* write orchestral music. In fact, he found orchestral writing quite difficult, which is partly why he waited so long before seriously attempting it. (He once said, 'A symphony is no joke!') He also wrote a lot of **chamber music** (music for a few instruments, such as a string quartet), about 200 songs, and a great deal of popular piano music.

Brahms (on the right) and the Viennese waltz composer Johann Strauss

Questions

1 Describe Brahms's family background.
2 Explain why Brahms changed his piano teacher when he was about ten years old.

This cartoon shows Brahms on his way to his favourite restaurant in Vienna, called 'The Red Hedgehog'

3 What was Brahms expected to do as the family was poor?

4 Where may Brahms have developed some bad manners as a young man?

5 What effect may the violinist Reményi have had on Brahms's music?

6 Explain how Joachim helped Brahms.

7 Give some reasons why Brahms is not always thought of as a romantic composer.

8 Explain what effect Brahms's teacher, Marxsen, had on him.

9 What is one of the differences between Brahms and some of the composers before him?

10 Why did one conductor call Brahms's first symphony 'Beethoven's 10th'?

Things to do

1 Here is the theme of the finale from Brahms's fourth symphony. The composer borrowed it from a Bach cantata, and turned it into a huge **passacaglia**. (This is a slow piece of music which keeps repeating the same tune moving between different parts.) Use this tune as a bass to make up some music of your own. First play it several times on the piano or a bass instrument, and then try to make up a melody which will go on top of it. When you have done this, listen to the beginning of the fourth movement to see how Brahms uses this tune.

2 Brahms wrote his four symphonies between the ages of 42 and 52. Many other composers wrote theirs earlier, and some even later. Design and make your own chart, showing the age at which the following composers wrote their first symphonies. You can find the information in this book:

   Beethoven, Mendelssohn, Berlioz, Schumann, Brahms.

3 Brahms did not find it easy to write orchestral music, especially symphonies. Try to put yourself in Brahms's shoes and think of all the things about writing orchestral music which worried him. For example, what is different about writing orchestral music, especially symphonies, and writing piano music or songs? When you have thought of some of these things, write an imaginary letter from Brahms to his friend Joachim, explaining his difficulties.

Wagner (1813–1883)

The German composer Richard Wagner

Richard Wagner was born in Leipzig, Germany, in May 1813. When he was only six months old his father died and his mother moved the family to Dresden. There she married an actor, Ludwig Geyer. This was not the only connection that Wagner had with the theatre at an early age: his sisters were on the stage, and Richard himself wrote many pieces of poetry and short plays, similar to those of the Greeks and Shakespeare which he enjoyed so much at school.

Wagner made the decision to become a composer quite early in his life, partly because he needed music for his plays. Not until he was 18, however, did he decide to have any lessons in composition.

Two years later Wagner tried to compose the type of piece that was eventually to make him famous: **opera**. For the next six years he had various jobs at opera houses in some of the smaller German cities, and this experience obviously helped him with his own writing. So far there was no great success for him, and in fact after a great deal of travelling, he and his wife arrived in Paris in 1839, having escaped from a lot of people to whom they owed money!

Wagner had hoped to put on a performance of *Rienzi* (one of his first operas) in Paris, but he was unsuccessful, and so was forced to write songs and arrange French music in order to make some money. He was certainly not able to live the luxurious life which he always thought he deserved, and which had helped to put him in debt.

His first success came at last in 1842 in Dresden, where *Rienzi* was performed. It was so popular that Wagner was appointed second conductor at the court opera. In 1845, the next opera *Tannhäuser* was performed, and two years later *Lohengrin*.

When Wagner was 35, he became involved in political unrest in Dresden, and because he was on the side of the people, rather than the government, he had to leave the country. He stayed with Liszt at Weimar, and then went to Switzerland, where in 1851 he became involved in his series of operas known as *The Ring*.

In 1857, when Wagner was 44, this enormous composition was interrupted. The composer fell in love with Mathilde Wesendonk, whose rich husband had lent him money and provided him with a house on his estate. Mathilde inspired the composition of *Tristan and Isolde*, a **music-drama** (Wagner now preferred this name to **opera**) which was completed partly in Venice in 1859, following Wagner's wife's return to Germany after a quarrel.

After two years spent in Paris, where Wagner still hoped for

The hero of Wagner's opera Siegfried (the third opera in the Ring cycle) kills his rival who has been changed into a dragon

Wagner with his wife Cosima, and his father-in-law Liszt, seated in the window

success, he returned to Germany with his wife, who had by now forgiven him. For the next few years he made money by giving orchestral concerts, but gradually got into more debt because of his extravagant life-style. He felt the world owed him luxuries, in return for the masterpieces he had given it!

Wagner's next opportunity was at the court of King Ludwig II of Bavaria, a young and mentally unstable ruler, who invited Wagner to become his personal friend and artistic adviser. Wagner had complete freedom as well as great influence at the court for the short time he was there. Eventually he had to leave, after the court officials (who disliked his extravagance) forced the King to send him away. While he was there, however, he had engaged Hans von Bülow as the court opera conductor, and fallen in love with the man's wife, Cosima. She was the daughter of the composer Liszt, and in 1870, when Wagner was 57, they were married. By this time Wagner's first wife had died.

Wagner's music

Wagner stands out as an unusual composer for a number of reasons. First, he concentrated on writing operas, and wrote the **libretto** (the words) of each one himself. Secondly, he gave a lot of attention to the orchestra's music in his later operas, as well as to the singers' parts. Thirdly, he wrote music for a much larger orchestra than was usually found in the opera house.

One of the most important features of his music was the use of what is called the **leitmotiv**, meaning 'leading motive'. This is a short musical phrase which was used to identify a character or an object, and which could be played in different ways whenever the character or object appeared in the opera.

The **leitmotiv** had been used in a much simpler form by composers before, including Berlioz in his *Fantastic Symphony* (see page 48), but never to the extent that it was used in Wagner's compositions.

The opera house at Bayreuth which Wagner had specially built to stage his operas

Questions

1. Why did Wagner's family move when he was only six months old?
2. Give one reason why Wagner decided to become a composer.
3. At what age did Wagner have composition lessons?
4. Why did Wagner go to Paris in 1839?
5. Describe Wagner's first musical success.
6. Explain why Wagner had to leave Germany when he was 35.

7 Explain how the composition of *Ring* cycle of operas was interrupted.

8 Why was Wagner often in debt?

9 Describe Wagner's connection with King Ludwig II of Bavaria.

10 Give one example of how Wagner's music is different from that of other opera composers.

Things to do

1 Here are two versions of the opening of the Prelude to *Tristan and Isolde* by Wagner. One has Wagner's own unusual **chromatic** harmony, and the other has a simple **diatonic** harmony. Ask your teacher to play both versions, and see if you can guess which is which. Discuss the differences with your teacher.

A romantic painting of the lovers Tristan and Isolde drinking a love potion

2 Design a chart which contains details of the main events in Wagner's life and career. It could begin like this:

Born:	May 1813
First composition lessons:	Aged 18
etc. . . .	

3 Wagner's life was a very full one. Imagine that you have to write his obituary in a newspaper (this is a short article about someone who has just died), but you only have space for 200 words. Try to fit in all the things that happened to the composer in that space.

Opera

An **opera** is like a musical play where most of the words are *sung* instead of spoken. Sometimes they are sung by the main characters in the story, and sometimes they are sung by a **chorus** (lots of people who sing together). These singers are accompanied by an orchestra. Occasionally the orchestra plays on its own, for example at the beginning of the opera, when we hear the **overture**.

The first great opera composer, Claudio Monteverdi   *Giacomo Puccini, the Italian composer of* Madam Butterfly

Apart from the story being told in song instead of speech, an opera is like any other production in the theatre: there has to be scenery; the singers wear costumes; and there are theatre lights. There is also a director of the opera, who is in charge, just as there is in a play.

When a composer writes an opera, the first thing that is needed is the **libretto**. This is the story for the opera, which the composer then sets to music. The libretto is rather like a play, and the writer of the libretto is called a **librettist**. Some composers, such as Wagner, have written their own libretti.

In most operas, composers wrote two sorts of part for the main singers: **arias** and **recitatives**. Arias are simply songs which occur regularly throughout the opera, while recitatives are a kind of singing which sounds rather like speaking; although the words have their own notes, there is no fixed rhythm, since the singer follows the natural rhythm of the words. In 17th and 18th century opera recitatives were often used to help the story of the opera move along quickly, while the aria was the opportunity to hear the singer's voice, and for the composer to express the feelings of the character in music. In later operas, the difference between the recitative and aria was less noticeable, and the music usually became more continuous.

The first operas were written around the year 1600 in Italy. The earliest ones only contained recitatives, but gradually composers added more interesting parts, such as arias, choruses and dances. Monteverdi (1567–1643) was one of the first composers to write operas in this way.

Opera soon became a popular form of entertainment in other countries. Henry Purcell (see page 7), the English composer, wrote several operas, including the well known *Dido and Aeneas* in 1689. From 1733, in Paris, the composer Rameau helped to establish a French style of opera.

Handel, Gluck and Mozart were the best known opera composers of the 18th century. Handel had worked in an opera house in Hamburg, and then spent four years in Italy before coming to London, where Italian opera was popular. His first operas were very successful, but later he concentrated on oratorios (see page 14). Gluck reformed opera in 1762, with his opera *Orpheus and Euridice*. He simplified the plot of the story and made the music fit the drama. Mozart developed some of Gluck's operatic ideas. Later, he turned opera into a great art in the 1780s, and seemed to make the characters of his stories almost come alive. Among his best known operas are *The Marriage of Figaro*, *The Magic Flute* and *Così fan Tutte*.

In the 19th century there were more opera composers than there had been before. Most of these, including Rossini and Verdi (you can read more about Verdi's operas on pages 65–6) concentrated on the music of the singers, and kept the orchestra mainly for accompanying them. Wagner, however, wrote operas in which the orchestra's part was quite important too (see page 60). In the same century operas began to be written which needed very elaborate costumes and scenery: these are called **grand operas**. They also contained ballets, and their subject was usually tragedy. Verdi's *Aida* is a good example of one. One of the best known operas of the 19th century is *Carmen*, by Bizet. It is set in Seville, Spain and tells the story of a girl from a cigarette factory, Carmen, a soldier, José, and a bull fighter called Escamillo. Despite its enormous popularity now it was not a great success at the time it was written, 1875.

In the 20th century composers have followed various styles of opera, and have used whichever best suited their story. Richard Strauss became world famous as an opera composer when he wrote *Salome* in 1905, and Puccini almost became a millionaire when he wrote *Madam Butterfly* in 1904. One of the most successful opera composers of the middle of this century was Benjamin Britten, who became famous in 1945 as the composer of *Peter Grimes*.

Questions

1 What does the word **opera** mean? Use your own words.
2 What is a **libretto**?
3 What is an **aria**?
4 What is a **recitative**?

The dramatic last moments of Carmen. *Don José stabs Carmen as the bullfighter Escamillo emerges from his victory in the bullring*

5 Describe the earliest operas, around the year 1600.
6 Name two opera composers of the 18th century.
7 In what ways did Gluck 'reform' opera?
8 In what way were Wagner's operas different from other 19th-century ones?
9 What was **grand opera**?
10 Name a 20th-century opera composer and one of his operas.

Things to do

Q. 1—see next page
2 Design and make a chart of the history of opera, divided into centuries. Each section should show the important opera composers of the century and the main operas.
3 Write an imaginary programme note for a performance of an opera of your choice. Write about the opera itself (you can find the information in a music reference book such as *The Oxford Junior Companion to Music* if necessary) and include a brief history of opera, written in your own words. If you have time you can include some facts about the composer too.

1   Here are the words and music of both an
aria and a recitative from an opera,
Mozart's *Don Giovanni*, printed separately.
Look at each, while your teacher plays the
music to you. When you think you know
which music goes with which words, copy
out the music, with the correct words
underneath.

You know now for certain
The name of the traitor
My honour who assaulted,
My father who murder'd;

'Tis indeed past believing that a crime so atrocious was the act of a
man of breeding!

ARIA

Andante (at a walking pace)

Donna Anna

RECITATIVE

Don Ottavio

Verdi (1813–1901)

Giuseppe Verdi was born in the village of Roncole, near the town of Parma, in Italy. His parents were poor, and Verdi did not have much opportunity to read books or study music. Fortunately there were several people who were happy to help him, such as the businessman Antonio Barezzi, who lived in the nearby town of Busseto, where Verdi went to school at the age of ten. Barezzi provided lodging for Verdi, and introduced him to the local orchestra, which rehearsed in his house. Verdi was also encouraged to practise Barezzi's piano.

When he was 14, Verdi wrote an overture which the local orchestra performed. Two years later he became the conductor's assistant and also wrote a symphony. He was soon sent to the Milan music college, which rejected him, and then went to work as a musician at the famous *La Scala* theatre. Here he heard all the standard operas of the day. When he returned to Busseto he was disappointed in not being given the job of cathedral organist, but he still started to work on his first opera *Oberto*.

When he was 25 Verdi returned once more to Milan, and was very lucky to have his opera performed at *La Scala* in the following year. He seemed to be an instant success. The director of the theatre offered him a contract for three more operas, and a music publisher decided to publish the successful opera's vocal score. Although he certainly did find success very quickly, Verdi soon became the victim of tragedy. The year after his first opera was produced, both his young children and his wife died. It was hardly surprising that his next opera was not a success.

Verdi wanted to give up composing altogether now, but the manager of *La Scala* gradually persuaded him to produce a new opera in 1842, based on the bible story of Nebuchadnezzar (*Nabucco*). It was an immediate success, and from this point onwards, Verdi turned out a stream of operas (26 altogether) and continued to compose even when he was quite old. In his 70s he led a life of semi-retirement on his estate at Sant' Agata, but still had success with his opera *Otello* in 1887 when he was 73, and with his last, *Falstaff*, which was produced when the composer was nearly 80. After this he really did retire, and died in 1901.

The Italian composer Giuseppe Verdi

The cover of a special issue of an Italian magazine marking the opening of Verdi's opera Falstaff

Verdi rehearsing the cast for his opera
The Masked Ball *in 1858*

Rigoletto, hunchback and court jester,
from a modern production of the opera

Verdi's music

It is interesting that both Verdi and Wagner (see page 59) were born in 1813, and that both composers concentrated on writing operas. They were however very different people, and their music was also different. Verdi had a particular gift for melody, and his operas are full of good tunes for the singers, whereas Wagner paid particular attention to his operas' orchestral music. Unlike Wagner, Verdi did not have anything very much to say about how operas ought to be written. He just wrote a great many!

Of Verdi's 26 operas, three of his most popular were written within a few years of each other, and these are among the most popular operas in the world today: *Rigoletto, Il Trovatore* and *La Traviata*. The first is about a court jester and his relationship with his master, while *Il Trovatore* is the story of a nobleman's son who has been brought up by a gipsy to be a troubadour. *La Traviata* was not a success at first, as the other two operas were, but soon became so after its first few performances. It is based on a book called *The Lady of the Camellias*, by Dumas.

Although Verdi was mainly an opera composer, he did write some other compositions too. The best known of these is his *Requiem*, a choral work with Latin words from the Requiem Mass set to music. It is a large concert piece for soloists, chorus and orchestra, in which trumpets are played off-stage, to herald the day of judgement!

The scene with the witches from Verdi's Macbeth, *based on Shakespeare's play*

Questions
1 Describe Verdi's background.
2 How did Antonio Barezzi help Verdi?
3 How old was Verdi when he wrote a symphony?
4 Describe Verdi's very sudden success at the age of 26.
5 What tragedy occurred for Verdi soon after his first success?
6 What operas did Verdi produce during his 'retirement'?
7 Which other composer was born in the same year as Verdi?
8 What is the connection between the two composers (see Q.7)?
9 What are the differences between the music of these two composers (see Q.7)?
10 Describe any one composition by Verdi which is *not* an opera.

Things to do
1 Next time you make up some music of your own in class, experiment with placing some instruments and players further away from most of the performers than usual, to try to get some special effect, just as Verdi did in his requiem. For example, you could try placing one player and instrument at the far end of the room from the other players, or even in a passage outside the classroom. Discuss the advantages or disadvantages of this kind of performance.
2 From the description of the opera *Il Trovatore*, which is included in this chapter, design a poster to advertise a production of this opera.
3 Read this chapter, and the chapter on Wagner (page 59) very carefully, and then write about 200 words comparing the two composers and their music.

Tchaikovsky (1840–1893)

The Russian composer Peter Tchaikovsky

Peter Tchaikovsky is probably the best known Russian composer. He had piano lessons at the age of four from his governess, and later his parents arranged for him to be taught by a piano teacher. Although he was a good performer, he was not good enough to earn his living as a professional concert pianist.

When he was 19, Tchaikovsky became a clerk, and stayed in his job for nearly four years. At the same time he began to have theory lessons from a professor at the new music conservatory (college) at St Petersburg. When he was 22 Tchaikovsky decided to take up music as a career, and entered the conservatory as a full time student. He was now very poor, and had to give some music lessons in order to make enough money to live. He also had lessons in **orchestration** (how to write music for an orchestra to play it) from Anton Rubinstein, the conservatory's director.

By the time he was 25, Tchaikovsky was offered a job teaching music in the Moscow conservatory, which was run by Anton Rubinstein's brother, Nicholas. There he was at least able to concentrate on composing without being so poor, although he found the work physically and mentally tiring. Three years later, the composer Balakirev suggested that Tchaikovsky should write his overture *Romeo and Juliet*, which he did the following year. This turned out to be one of his finest and most popular compositions. In the same year (1868) he became engaged to an opera singer, but she left Tchaikovsky very suddenly, and while she was on tour married another man.

Tchaikovsky's first real success as a composer came with his piano concerto, still a very popular piece of music. It was dedicated to Nicholas Rubinstein, but after Rubinstein had been very rude about the work, the composer not surprisingly dedicated it to another musician, the conductor Hans von Bülow (see *Wagner*, page 60). Von Bülow was pleased with the concerto, and conducted its first performance in the USA in 1875.

Two years later, Tchaikovsky unwisely allowed himself to be persuaded into marrying a girl whom he did not love. She wrote to him quite suddenly, telling him that she had fallen in love with him while she had been a student at the conservatory where he taught. After only a month he realized that the marriage was a failure. He left the girl, and saved himself from a nervous breakdown, though she finished her life in a mental home.

Tchaikovsky's house near Moscow, now a museum

At about the same time, however, Tchaikovsky was very fortunate to receive another letter, this time from a very wealthy lady called Madame von Meck. She admired his music so much that she wanted to give him enough money to allow him to spend all his time composing. Her only condition was that the two of them should never meet each other. He was now able to complete his opera, *Eugene Onegin*, and his fourth symphony, which he dedicated to Madame von Meck.

The rest of Tchaikovsky's life was filled with travel and success in other countries, including England (where he received an honorary degree of Doctor of Music at Cambridge) and the USA. On his return from England in 1893, he conducted the first performance of his sixth symphony, which he called the *Pathétique* (meaning pathetic). This work is full of the composer's own sense of self pity and disappointment. Shortly afterwards he died—almost certainly by suicide, and not, as is commonly stated, from cholera after drinking a glass of unboiled water.

The Blue Bird from the ballet Sleeping Beauty

Tchaikovsky's music

Tchaikovsky is without doubt a romantic composer, and much of his music is very emotional and sentimental. His *Pathétique* symphony is a good example of this. Because Tchaikovsky allowed his feelings to take control of his compositions, there sometimes seems to have been little or no planned design behind them. The result was that they often had no form, as he himself admitted. He could compose superb melodies and harmonies, and organize combinations of instruments to produce brilliant effects of tone-colour, but so often his emotions seemed completely to take over the music. Some of his orchestral pieces are just a succession of episodes (sections) with no overall pattern. For example, the first tune of his Piano Concerto No. 1 is never heard again after the opening.

There are of course many positive aspects of Tchaikovsky's orchestral writing, particularly the symphonies, which show him as an original and individual composer. The opening of the fourth symphony is one example, where after a loud entry of horns, bassoons, trombones, and tuba, we hear a sudden and exciting change of key when the trumpets and woodwind come in. Another example can be found later in that symphony, where there is a whole movement played *pizzicato* on the strings. The sixth symphony, which has its third movement unusually in 5/4 time, is the first one to end

A page from a sketch for the second movement of Tchaikovsky's sixth symphony 'The Pathétique'

A scene from Tchaikovsky's opera
The Queen of Spades

by fading out very quietly. Previously, symphonies usually ended very definitely, with plenty of loud chords.

Tchaikovsky wrote some of the most successful of all ballet music, including the *Sleeping Beauty*, *Nutcracker* and *Swan Lake*. Since this music is designed for dancers, it has a built-in form of its own.

As well as his six symphonies, three piano concertos and violin concerto, Tchaikovsky also wrote several operas including *Eugene Onegin* and *The Queen of Spades*, church music, songs and chamber music. One of his best known pieces is the *1812 Overture*.

Questions

1 Who first taught Tchaikovsky the piano?
2 At what age, and for how long, did Tchaikovsky become a clerk?
3 What extra music lessons did Tchaikovsky have while he was a clerk?
4 Describe Tchaikovsky's life as a student.
5 What job was Tchaikovsky offered when he was 25?
6 What is the connection between the composer Balakirev and an overture of Tchaikovsky's?
7 How did Rubinstein react to the piece of music which Tchaikovsky dedicated to him?
8 Why was Tchaikovsky eventually able to spend all of his time composing?
9 In your own words, describe Tchaikovsky's music. What are its faults?
10 Give some examples of the unusual aspects of Tchaikovsky's music.

*Tchaikovsky played on this piano
when he was a boy*

Things to do

1a In the opening of Tchaikovsky's fourth symphony there is a sudden change of key, and this creates an unusual and exciting effect in the music. Next time you make up some music of your own in class, try to change key suddenly. To help you do this, you could experiment with the ideas below, by only using the notes suggested for each of the three keys given. As soon as you change from one box of notes to another, you have changed key.

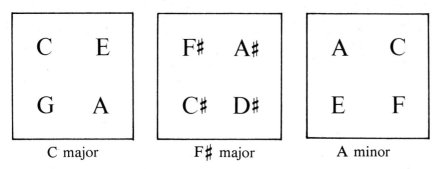

C major   F♯ major   A minor

1b In the melody below, two bars of the music could be written *three notes lower*, in another key. Listen to your teacher playing it to decide where this should be, and then re-write the whole melody with the part you have chosen changed. Ask your teacher to play the new version. Does it sound right? If not, try again.

2 In the section on Sonatas and Symphonies there is a diagram representing sonata form (page 41). Design and draw a simple diagram of your own which represents the kind of form Tchaikovsky sometimes used, of different *episodes* (this means different sections of music put one after the other). You could give each episode a letter name.

3 Imagine how Tchaikovsky felt when he received the letter from Madame von Meck, described in this chapter. Write a letter of reply, as you think Tchaikovsky might have written it.

Nationalism

Nationalism is about feeling patriotic, or being very interested in your country. Nationalism in music is a name that has been given to a special way in which many composers have written their music. Instead of just writing what we sometimes call **absolute** music (music which does not tell a story or have any particular meaning) these composers wrote music which was connected with their own country. One of the ways they did this was to include their countries' folk music in their compositions.

Nationalism in music started in the Romantic period of musical history (see page 30). Before this, Baroque and Classical music had mainly been absolute music, and had not expressed feelings or emotions in an obvious way. But Romantic music *did* do this, and used a much greater variety of rhythms and melodies to express emotions, sometimes vividly. It's not surprising perhaps that one of the emotions these composers wanted to express was a strong

feeling of patriotism, especially in the 19th century: this was a time when many people in Europe began to feel very loyal to their country.

Schumann, Chopin and Liszt were among the earliest nationalists. Schumann did not show this much in his actual compositions, but he was very interested in German books and music from an early age. Chopin (see page 50), who was half Polish and half French, used Polish dance rhythms, and Liszt (see page 31) expressed the gipsy music of Hungary in his 19 Hungarian Rhapsodies for the piano.

Composers who were born a little later were more obviously nationalistic, and are more usually thought of as nationalistic composers. Two who came from what was then called Bohemia (now part of Czechoslovakia) were Dvořák (see page 75) and Smetana. Dvořák's *Gipsy Songs*, *Dumky Trio* and overture *My Home* are all connected with his home country.

Bela Bartók and Zoltán Kodály were two composers whose nationalism came from an interest in the folk music of their own country,

Liszt, composer of Hungarian rhapsodies, playing to an audience

The Hungarian composer Bartók listening over headphones to some recorded folk tunes

A Hungarian musician playing a folk tune on a fipple flute, an instrument rather like a recorder

The Finnish composer Jean Sibelius

Hungary. From 1905, both went around collecting folk songs and tunes which had been handed down over the years. Bartók's music is often percussive and dissonant. One of his best known pieces is his *Concerto for Orchestra*. Kodály is well known for his opera suite *Háry János*, and for devising a method of training young musicians called the Kodály Method.

Scandinavia has produced two well known nationalists: Grieg in Norway and Sibelius in Finland. Grieg's pieces include such titles as *Norwegian Peasant March* and *Norwegian Bridal Procession*, while many of Sibelius's titles have been taken from the Finnish folk history (the *Kalevala*). One of his best known pieces is actually called *Finlandia*.

The Norwegian composer Edvard Grieg

One of the most famous groups of nationalist composers is often just called *The Five*: Balakirev, Cui, Borodin, Mussorgsky and Rimsky-Korsakov, who were all Russian. Borodin's opera *Prince Igor* and Mussorgsky's *Boris Godunov* are both based on Russian history, while Rimsky-Korsakov's music shows the influence of his country upbringing, which must have taught him many folk songs. Another Russian nationalist is Glinka, whose opera *A Life for the Czar* is based on the invasion of Russia by the Poles in 1613.

A very different group of nationalist composers came from Spain: Albéniz, Granados and De Falla. De Falla was very interested in Spanish folk songs, and organized festivals to try to get others interested too. One of his pieces was entitled *Nights in the Gardens of Spain*. Granados founded a school of music at Barcelona, where he was director until his death. One of his sets of piano pieces, *Goyescas*, is based on pictures by the Spanish painter Goya.

In Britain a nationalistic trend in composing began towards the end of the 19th century. The composers Parry, Mackenzie and Stanford showed the characteristics of their countries (England, Scotland and Ireland respectively) in their music. Stanford was a professor of music at Cambridge and a teacher at the Royal College of Music. Among his pupils was Vaughan Williams, who collected English folk songs and used them in his own compositions.

Questions

1   What does **nationalism** mean?
2   What is one way in which composers have made their music nationalistic?
3   Why did nationalism in music not occur until the romantic period?
4   Name some early nationalists in music.
5   Name one nationalist composer from Czechoslovakia.
6   Who were the Scandinavian nationalists, and what were the names of some of their pieces?
7   Who were 'The Five'?
8   Name some Spanish nationalist composers. Which one founded a music school?
9   Who were the early British nationalists?
10   Give one reason why Vaughan Williams's music is nationalistic.

Things to do

1   Next time you make up a piece of music in class, try to construct it from the folk songs that you know. Here are some titles of well known folk songs:

Blow the Man Down	Family of Man
The Foggy Dew	Home Sweet Home
The Big Ship Sails	Last Thing on my
Blaydon Races	Mind
Casey Jones	Scarborough Fair
Drunken Sailor	

You could start by simply putting a few bars of different folk songs together just to see what the result is. If you can't make up your own music, then use some tunes from a book of folk songs. Mix up different parts from a number of songs, and copy the result on to manuscript paper. Get your teacher to play this, and then see if you can improve it.

2   Design a poster for your classroom wall showing all the nationalist composers mentioned in this chapter. Group them according to their country, and try to include as much information as you can.

3   Write about the three earliest nationalists mentioned in this chapter. You can find out more about them by looking at their individual chapters in this book. Try in particular to find out more about *how* or *why* they were nationalistic, and concentrate on this part of their work. The title of your piece of writing could be, *The Early Nationalist Composers*.

Dvořák (1841–1904)

Antonín Dvořák (pronounced Dvorshak) was born in Bohemia, a country now known as Czechoslovakia. His father was the village innkeeper and butcher, as well as an amateur musician. Dvořák's early musical education was based on his local church, where he was a choirboy from the age of eight. When he was 12 he was sent to live with an uncle in a nearby town, where he went to school and had proper music lessons.

By the time Dvořák was 14 he was expected to join his father's business, but after two years the man realized that his son was better suited to a career in music. At the age of 16 Dvořák went to the Organ School at Prague. Here he continued to play the violin and keyboard instruments, and also had some lessons in composition.

After two years, however, Dvořák's father was no longer able to pay his son's allowance, and so Dvořák now had to leave the school and make his own living. For the next twelve years he did this by playing the viola in an orchestra, and by teaching. During this time he also played for the Czech National Theatre and made friends with other musicians, including the composer Smetana, who became the theatre's conductor in 1866.

By the time Dvořák was 30 he decided to give up orchestral playing and concentrate on composition. He married one of the singers from the chorus of the Czech Theatre, and he lived off the money he made as a church organist. When he was 34, Dvořák's music came to the attention of the composer Brahms (see page 56), who recommended that Dvořák be given a grant by the Austrian government. Brahms also found someone to publish Dvořák's *Moravian Dances*. But just as Dvořák was beginning to become known as a composer, his success was spoilt by the death of one of his children in 1876.

Dvořák's *Stabat Mater* (a choral work based on old Latin words) and *Slavonic Dances* made him known in Europe, and when he was 43 he was invited to London for a performance of the *Stabat Mater* at the

The Czech composer Antonín Dvořák

Dvořák and his family on the steps of their home in New York

A scene from one of Dvořák's operas
The Peasant a Rogue

Title page of The Devil and Kate

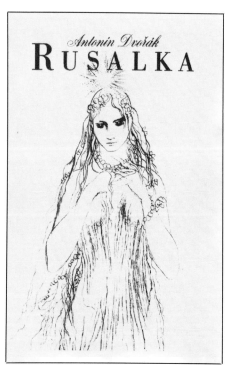

Title page of Rusalka

Albert Hall. This success encouraged him to write more choral music, and he returned to England several times for performances of these pieces, including his *Requiem* in 1891.

The following year, when he was 51, Dvořák went to New York to be the director of the National Music Conservatory. Although he only stayed there for three years, he wrote his well known 'New World' symphony and *Cello Concerto* during this time. He returned to Prague to teach at the Conservatory, and in 1901 he was made its director. He died three years later.

Dvořák's music

Czechoslovakia has always been rich in folk music, and Dvořák's compositions were influenced by this tradition. For example, in many of his pieces he used Czeck dances, such as the **polka**, **furient**, **dumka** and **styrienne**. Dvořák also came into contact with Czeck history through the operas of Smetana, and this may well have influenced his music too. Perhaps the most patriotic sounding of all Dvořák's pieces are his *Slavonic Dances* and *Slavonic Rhapsodies*.

Dvořák wrote nine symphonies altogether (the same number as Beethoven wrote), but there is some confusion about the way they are numbered. Dvořák seems to have been careful to avoid having anything published which he did not feel was very good. His first four symphonies were not published in his own lifetime, and so the fifth to the ninth became numbered by the publisher as the first to the fifth. To complicate matters further, these were not even numbered in the order in which they were written, because Dvořák revised the first of these (really his fifth) after he had written his next two, and called it his third. His best known symphony is the fifth (really his ninth), called 'From the New World', and was written while he was in America. Although it is often thought that this contains some actual Indian or Negro music, this is not true. Dvořák's own tunes simply sound American to many people.

Dvořák wrote a great deal of choral music, and had a lot of success with it, particularly in England. He also wrote ten operas, the most successful of which, *Rusalka* and *The Devil and Kate*, were composed towards the end of his life. He also wrote chamber music, such as the 'Slavonic' string quartet (he wrote ten quartets) and the Piano Quintet in A major. Some of his best chamber music was written towards the end of his life: the 'American' string quartet, his last two string quartets, and the 'Dumky' piano trio which contains six examples of the *dumka* Czech dance.

Questions

1 Where did Dvořák receive his early musical education?
2 What might Dvořák have ended up doing instead of music?
3 What forced Dvořák to leave the Prague organ school?
4 How did Dvořák make a living after he left the Prague organ school?
5 In what ways did Brahms help Dvořák?
6 With which kind of music was Dvořák most successful in England?
7 Describe one of the influences on Dvořák's music.
8 Explain why Dvořák's symphonies are sometimes numbered 1–9, and sometimes 1–5.
9 Which is Dvořák's best known symphony, and how did it get its title?
10 Describe the other kinds of music that Dvořák wrote.

Things to do

1 Here is a well known tune from the 'New World' symphony by Dvořák, with all the bars printed in the wrong order, except for the first one. Play the bars on a classroom instrument or get someone else to, and try to fit them in the right order.

Largo (slow and dignified)

2 Design a travel poster about Czech music. It should contain information about Czechslovakia's two most important composers, Dvořák and Smetana. You will find the information you need in this chapter, although you can also find out more about Smetana by looking in a music reference book, such as *The Oxford Junior Companion to Music*.

3 Write a concert programme note about Dvořák's 'New World' symphony. It should contain a very short account of his life and all the information about the symphony, including the different numbers it is known by and the reasons for this confusion.

Debussy (1862–1918)

The French composer Claude Debussy

Debussy with his daughter in 1916

Claude Debussy was born at St Germain-en-Laye, not far from Paris. His parents owned a china shop there, but after three years the family moved nearer to the city, and Debussy's father found a new job.

Although Debussy did not go to school, his mother taught him to read and write, and he had piano lessons from an elderly Italian. When the boy was nine years old he was encouraged by another teacher (who had been a pupil of Chopin) to take the entrance exam of the Paris Conservatoire (college) of Music. She even gave him piano lessons free of charge, and within only a few months Debussy had passed.

Debussy remained at the Conservatoire for eleven years, and gained quite a reputation for not taking any notice of the accepted rules about composing music. When his teacher asked him why he composed unusual-sounding music, Debussy simply said, 'Because it sounds nice'.

When he was still at the Conservatoire, at the age of 18, Madame von Meck (the millionairess who had admired Tchaikovsky's music) asked Debussy to be her 'family musician' for three years. She wanted him to teach her children and to play for her. Debussy travelled with the family a great deal in the summers of these three years, and met many people, including the composer Wagner.

Despite Debussy's unusual compositions, he won the Conservatoire's *Prix de Rome* in 1884. This entitled him to three years' study in Rome, during which time he was expected to write some music. But when he returned to Paris he was told by the judges that his music was too unusual to be publicly performed!

Debussy settled down to life as a professional composer, although for the first few years he found it very difficult to make much money, especially since he disliked teaching. He had to rely on being given work by publishers, such as arranging other people's music, or writing music in which he wasn't really interested. He also received money from friends.

It was not until 1900, when Debussy was 38, that he really began to be noticed as a composer. Some of his music was heard at the Paris Exhibition, and two years later his opera, *Pelléas et Mélisande*, was performed in Paris and was a great success. In another two years Debussy divorced his wife Lilly (who later attempted suicide because of this) and married Emma Bardac, the wife of a wealthy man. Debussy was soon in demand as a pianist and conductor, and continued to compose in spite of illness. He died in 1918, the last year of the First World War.

Debussy's music

Debussy was the first important composer to write music after the romantic composers of the 19th century: he was the first **Impressionist**. The Impressionists were not very concerned with the *form* of classical music, or the *drama* of romantic music; they were not even interested in their music telling a story. Their main concern was the *sound*, and if this was right, then the music was right.

Impressionism is not just about music. Most people think of French painters when they talk about Impressionists. The artist Monet is considered the founder of the Impressionist school of painters, and thought that light was the most important thing in a picture. Instead of painting an ordinary picture, Impressionists painted what looked like impressions of things: these often seem like blurred or hazy images.

Debussy used a number of new musical ideas to achieve his impressionism in music. One was discords. For example, when you hear this chord on the piano

you usually expect it to be followed by this one.

But Debussy might simply write several of the first type of chord, one after the other, without 'finishing off' any of them:

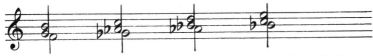

Another device which Debussy used was the **whole tone** scale. This is a scale which has no semitones in it, unlike any major or minor scale. The whole tone scale has an eerie effect, and creates the atmosphere of suspense and mistiness which so appealed to the impressionists.

One of Debussy's best known pieces is the *Prélude à l'après-midi d'un faune*. This was written when he was 30, and was based on a poem by Mallarmé. Another of his well known pieces is *La Mer*, which consists of three symphonic sketches that are intended to give the impression

Cartoon of Debussy conducting

This beautiful Japanese painting ('Golden fish') inspired Debussy to write a piano piece with the same title

Title page of Debussy's orchestral piece, La mer

of the sea. This was the closest Debussy got to a symphony. Debussy also wrote a lot of music for the piano, including the well known pieces *Claire de Lune* and *Golliwog's Cakewalk*. He also wrote many songs, and towards the end of his life composed some chamber music.

Questions

1 Which capital city was near Debussy's birthplace?
2 What is the connection between Debussy and Chopin?
3 Where did Debussy study music when he was ten?
4 What kind of reputation did Debussy have at the Conservatoire?
5 What is the connection between Debussy and Tchaikovsky?
6 Give one reason why Debussy had little money when he first started professional composition.
7 What kind of work did Debussy do at this time?
8 What was the connection between Debussy and the painter Monet?
9 Describe two musical devices that Debussy used in his compositions.
10 Describe Debussy's piece *La Mer*.

Things to do

1 Try to use the two lines of chords and notes on page 79 to make up a short piece of music of your own. You could use the chords in any pattern or order that you like, with each person in your group playing one note of each chord. You could also use the whole tone scale in any pattern that you like.
2 Can music or sound create an impression in *your* mind? Try this experiment. Get someone (it could be your teacher) to play several very different sounds or phrases on the piano, and as soon as you hear each one, draw your 'impression' of it on paper. It doesn't have to be a work of art, but whatever you draw should be what you think the music 'looks' like. Afterwards compare your drawings with those of other pupils in your class. Did you all get the same impression or not?
3a *In your own words*, explain what **Impressionism** is in music.
3b Look in an art book in your school library, or in the public library, and find the names of some impressionist painters and some of the pictures they painted. Write down their names and a short note about one or two of their pictures. If you live in a big city, visit your local art gallery and see it if has any paintings of the Impressionist School. Collect postcards and start a scrapbook.

Stravinsky (1882–1971)

Igor Stravinsky was born at a town near St Petersburg (now called Leningrad) in Russia. Unlike many Russians, his parents were quite well off. Rather than encourage Igor to become a musician, they sent him to the local university to study law. Stravinsky's father was an opera singer, and so Igor naturally grew up in a musical atmosphere. After he had been to university he began a legal career, but spent a lot of his spare time involved in music.

Once his father had died, Stravinsky felt free to give up law altogether. In 1902 he showed some of his compositions to Rimsky-Korsakov, a well known Russian composer who taught at the St Petersburg Conservatory of Music. The composer agreed to give Stravinsky composition lessons for the next three years.

Stravinsky's greatest opportunity came when he was 27. The ballet producer Serge Diaghilev heard some of his compositions, and asked him to write the music for a new ballet he was preparing, called *The Firebird*. It was produced a year later and was a great success. As a result, Diaghilev asked Stravinsky to write the music for *Petrushka* the following year. In this ballet, about puppets, Stravinsky showed how he could use rhythms and harmonies in an unusual and often daring way.

Stravinsky's most exciting ballet, however, was his third. In 1913 he wrote *The Rite of Spring*, and when it was first performed on stage in Paris it caused a sensation. Its harsh sounds and violent rhythms shocked people so much that there was almost a riot. A year later the First World War broke out, and this had an effect on the kinds of ballet which were produced. They could no longer be expensive or large, and did not need large orchestras.

Stravinsky decided to move to Switzerland. After the Russian revolution of 1917 he did not go back to his native country, but spent the next part of his life in Europe. When the Second World War broke out in 1939 he went to America, and in 1945 he became an American citizen.

A drawing of Stravinsky by Picasso

Stravinsky's music

One of the most unusual things about Stravinsky's music as a whole is its variety. Unlike many composers who have a style of their own, Stravinsky was never happy to write the same kind of music for very long, however successful it was. For example, after he had a great

The prince and the firebird from Stravinsky's ballet The Firebird

Stravinsky (with cigar) and artists Cocteau (left) and Picasso in the south of France in the 1920s

Stravinsky composing

A wild scene from Stravinsky's ballet The Rite of Spring

success with his ballets, he started to write smaller pieces of music, such as *The Soldier's Tale* in 1918, which is written for a small group of instrumentalists. During the next few years he composed several other smaller pieces, such as the ballet *Pulcinella* for voice and small orchestra. For a while Stravinsky was even influenced by jazz.

During these years Stravinsky was experimenting with **neo-classical** composition (this means 'new classical' music). He was trying to compose classical sounding music while using some modern ideas as well. People noticed this sort of music in particular, because many other composers, such as Schoenberg (see page 91), were experimenting with unusual modern (**avant-garde**) techniques which Stravinsky did not like. However, in the last few years of his life, he too wrote some pieces which used the twelve-note system of composition.

Stravinsky's best known works include the ballets mentioned above, *Oedipus Rex* (an opera-oratorio), the *Symphony of Psalms* for chorus and orchestra, as well as several concertos. He was one of the most important of all the 20th-century composers, and has had a great influence on people who are still writing music today.

Questions

1 Describe Stravinsky's family background.
2 When was Stravinsky able to study music full-time?
3 Which composer taught Stravinsky?
4 What lucky opportunity did Stravinsky have when he was 27?
5 What piece of music written by Stravinsky nearly caused a riot?
6 Explain why Stravinsky wrote no more large ballets for Diaghilev.
7 What is unusual about Stravinsky's music as a whole?
8 Describe how some of Stravinsky's pieces were different from his early large scale ballets.
9 Explain what is meant by **neo-classical** music.
10 Describe the other styles of music that Stravinsky experimented with.

Things to do

1 Here are the opening two bars of Stravinsky's *Rite of Spring*, printed in the original clef. Try to write this music out again, using an ordinary treble clef. You will need to put all the notes *eight notes lower* on the stave. The first bar has been done for you.

2 Imagine what it would be like if the first performance of a piece of music today had the same effect as *The Rite of Spring* had on its audience in 1913. Write a short newspaper report about this, with a suitable headline.

3 There are two Russian composers featured in this book: Stravinsky and Tchaikovsky. (a) Read about both of them, and try to write about their differences and similarities. (b) Try to find out about the following Russian composers, by using a music reference book (such as *The Oxford Junior Companion to Music*): Balakirev, Cui, Borodin, Mussorgsky and Rimsky-Korsakov. What are the connections between them?

American music

When the 'Pilgrim Fathers' sailed to America over 300 years ago, England was an important centre for music: the great English madrigal composers, such as William Byrd and Orlando Gibbons were alive (see page 4); English composers and performers were in great demand in Europe, both in churches and at the royal courts; London was considered to be the best place to learn the **viola da gamba** (a popular instrument of the time) and so students came from many countries to learn to play it.

Although England was a musical country at this time, the early Americans (who came from England) did not seem to have much time for musical activities. Perhaps that is not surprising, since these first settlers probably had plenty of other things to do. Partly as a result of this, American music took much longer to develop than music in Europe. Another reason for this was that there were no royal courts in America to encourage music, and very little church music. Yet in Europe, many of the great composers that you can read about in this book relied upon princes or churches to employ them.

However, by the 18th century, musical activity in America had begun to spread. Welsh, German and Swedish settlers brought their love of music to the state of Pennsylvania; a town called Bethlehem was founded by people from Bohemia, and soon had an orchestra and an organ playing in its church; New Orleans had a small opera company which was formed by French settlers; in New England, many books of psalm tunes appeared, and societies for singing psalms were founded.

In the 19th century there was a large increase in the immigrant population of America, most of whom came from Europe. Because of the political troubles in Germany in 1848, many Germans fled as far as America, and some of these must have been musical. As a result, there was a great deal more musical activity, much of which took place in musical societies such as the *Handel and Haydn Society* of Boston in 1815.

Another completely different musical influence which began in the 19th century was American negro slave music. Negro spirituals, and later the styles of Ragtime, Blues and Jazz all had an effect not only on popular music in the 20th century, but on other composers too; for example, Debussy's *Golliwog's Cakewalk* is based on Ragtime.

Charles Ives   *George Gershwin*

One of the first American composers to become well known in recent years was Charles Ives (1874–1954). He was an insurance agent who composed in his spare time. He knew that he could never make a living out of his music, partly because it was so unusual: for example, he liked to mix different tunes and sounds together at the same time. Listening to a piece by him is rather like walking down a street and hearing different music from people's houses!

One of the best known 20th-century American composers is Aaron Copland (born 1900). He always wanted to write music which would 'sound American', and so he was

A scene from Copland's ballet Billy the Kid

influenced by jazz, and other American popular music at first. Then he used folk music to help his compositions gain an American flavour, and in the 1950s he became interested in **Twelve-note composition** (see page 92). The music of Copland's 'middle period', is his most popular, especially the ballets *Billy the Kid* and *Rodeo*.

George Gershwin (1898–1937) started composing popular songs when he was about 15, and by the time he was 21 he had his first 'hit' with *Swanee*, which sold over two million copies. Like Jerome Kern, the successful composer of popular songs and musical comedies, he soon became established as a highly successful Broadway composer; but instead of just writing popular music, Gershwin tried to combine popular music and jazz with the 'classical' sounds of the symphony orchestra. His first piece in this new style, *Rhapsody in Blue* was an immediate success. Later he wrote *An American in Paris*, and an opera, *Porgy and Bess*.

Other well known American composers include Sousa (1854–1933), MacDowell (1861–1908) and Bernstein (born 1918).

Questions

1 How 'musical' a country was England 300 years ago?
2 Name two English madrigal composers.
3 Where was the best place to learn the viola da gamba 300 years ago?
4 Give one reason for the early American settlers' lack of interest in music.
5 Describe any one of the first musical activities in America in the 18th century.
6 Which European composer wrote a piece based on Ragtime?
7 Why couldn't Charles Ives make a living out of his compositions?
8 How did Aaron Copland give his compositions an 'American flavour'?
9 What is **Twelve-note composition**?
10 What new way of composing did Gershwin try, and how successful was it?

Things to do

1 *Rhapsody in Blue*, by George Gershwin, got its name from the style of music called **Blues**. In Blues melodies, the 3rd, 5th and 7th notes of the scale are usually *flattened*, producing a scale like the one below. Next time you make up some classroom music, try to do so using only these notes:

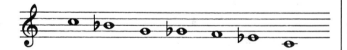

2 Make a chart of American history and music. Find out the main events in American history (ask you history teacher for help with this) and list them in order on one side of your chart. (You could include the well known presidents here, for example.) One the right hand side include some of the information in this chapter.
3 Look in a music reference book, such as *The Oxford Junior Companion to Music*, and try to find out something about the three composers mentioned at the very end of this chapter. Write down *in your own words* what you discover about them.

The English composer Benjamin Britten

Britten (1913–1976)

Benjamin Britten was born at Lowestoft in Suffolk. He began to compose at the early age of five, and when he was seven he started to learn the piano. A few years later he was taught the viola, and by the time he was 12 he was having lessons in composition from Frank Bridge, who was himself an established composer at that time. By now Britten had already written six string quartets and ten piano sonatas!

When he was 17 Britten won a scholarship to the Royal College of Music in London, where his new composition teacher was John Ireland. Britten soon became known as the composer of a piece called *Sinfonietta*. When he was 21 he wrote his first important choral work, *A Boy was Born*, and began to earn his living as a composer of film music. He worked for the G.P.O. film unit, and wrote the music for more than 20 documentary films.

His first success as a composer was when he wrote *Variations on a Theme of Frank Bridge* in 1937. Two years later, when the Second World War broke out, Britten went to live in New York. He returned to England in 1942, and within three years became well known for his opera *Peter Grimes*. This success encouraged him to write several more operas in the next few years (one opera a year from 1945–1949!).

In 1948, when Britten was 35, he started a music festival in the fishing village where he lived. The Aldeburgh Festival, as it is known, is now world famous, and international performers appear there every year.

Benjamin Britten received many honours during his lifetime, in recognition of his being the most successful British composer of the 20th century. In 1953 he was made a Companion of Honour; in 1965 he became a member of the Order of Merit; and in 1976, the year he died, he was made Lord Britten of Snape.

Britten's music

Many composers who lived in the 20th century are thought of as very 'modern' composers. Sometimes they are called **avant-garde** (see page 94) which means that they were leaders of a particular style of music before it was fully established. John Cage is this kind of composer, and was born the year before Britten.

Benjamin Britten, however, was not an avant-garde composer. Although his music is highly individual, he usually used fairly

The fisherman Peter Grimes and his apprentice, in a scene from Britten's opera set in a Suffolk fishing village

traditional ideas and methods in his compositions, such as ordinary chords or scales. But he put these ideas together in unusual ways which often surprised people. While composers such as Schoenberg and Webern were experimenting with **atonal** (12-tone) music earlier in the century, Britten managed to find new ways of using traditional tonality many years later.

Britten wrote many different kinds of music: operas (both large and small), church parables (church operas), orchestral pieces and songs. Among his most successful pieces are the opera *Peter Grimes* and the *War Requiem*. He also wrote many compositions for children, such as the *Young Person's Guide to the Orchestra* (based on a theme of Purcell), *Let's Make an Opera* and *Noye's Fludde*.

A scene from Brittens children's opera, Noye's Fludde

Questions

1 Where was Britten born?
2 At what age did Britten start having piano lessons?
3 Who taught Britten composition at the Royal College of Music?
4 Which two important pieces had Britten written by the time he was 21?
5 How did Britten first earn his living as a composer?
6 What piece of music written by Britten was concerned with his first composition teacher?
7 Where did Britten live from 1939–1942?
8 What kind of compositions did Britten write from 1945–1949?
9 Describe the Aldeburgh Festival.
10 What honours did Britten receive during his lifetime?

Things to do

1 Benjamin Britten wrote the music for over 20 films. Using whatever instruments are available to you, try to compose and perform music which would go well with a short poem or play. Your English teacher will be able to help you find some suitable words to start with.
2 Look through this book to find out when the following composers lived, and make a chart which shows this information. Then find out which of these composers have shocked or surprised audiences with their unusual music. Does your chart tell you anything?

Schoenberg; Stravinsky; Britten; Stockhausen.
3 Imagine you have to write about Benjamin Britten's life and music on the back of one of his record covers. Write this in not more than 200 words.

Britten with the conductor André Previn

British music

Although history of British music goes back to about the 11th century, when composition began in Britain, it was not until the 16th and early 17th centuries that England became a *leading* musical country. At that time composers such as Thomas Morley and William Byrd wrote madrigals and church music that has been popular ever since.

In the late 17th century the best known composer in England was Henry Purcell (see page 7), but by the 18th century England was no longer the important centre of music that it had been. The best known English composer of this time was Thomas Arne, who will always be remembered as the composer of *Rule, Britannia*. Handel (see page 13), who was very successful in this century, was a German who had simply chosen to live in England.

At the beginning of the 19th century an Irish composer called John Field (1782–1837) began an original style of composition for the piano which even influenced the famous Polish composer, Chopin. But it was not until later in the 19th century that British music looked as if it might improve. The composers Sullivan, Parry, Stanford and Mackenzie all contributed to the improved musical scene in Britain. Other composers, such as John Stainer and S. S. Wesley, concentrated on church music.

By the end of the 19th century the most famous English composer was Edward Elgar (1857–1934). His father and uncle ran a music shop just outside Worcester, and all his family were musical. He was so enthusiastic about anything to do with music that he almost taught himself all he knew. He was over 40 before he became well known as a composer. His first success was the *Enigma Variations*, still a popular

The English composer Edward Elgar

favourite, and during the next 20 years he wrote choral works, a cello concerto and two symphonies.

Frederick Delius (1862–1934) was five years younger than Elgar. His father was a wealthy

Frederick Delius, who lived in France and was blind for the last eight years of his life

wool merchant, and was able to establish Delius as an orange grower in Florida. After learning composition there, the composer persuaded his father to let him study music at Leipzig, and from the age of 26 he lived in Paris, where he composed a great deal. Eventually he settled with his wife in a nearby village, where for the last ten years of his life he was blind and paralysed. Among his best known orchestral pieces are *On Hearing the First Cuckoo in Spring* and *Brigg Fair*.

Ralph Vaughan Williams (1872–1958) was born ten years after Delius. He went to the Royal College of Music and later studied abroad. When he was about 40 he began to write music in his own particular style, of which his *Fantasia on a theme of Thomas Tallis* is a popular example. His music includes no less

A pastoral set design for Vaughan William's ballet Job

Ralph Vaughan Williams, who wrote a lot of music based on English folk songs

than nine symphonies, four operas and a ballet.

One of the first British composers born in the 20th century was Sir William Walton (born 1902), who taught himself composition. His best known piece, *Façade*, was written when he was only 21; it consists of poems recited against Walton's often humorous music. His other music includes two operas, two symphonies, concertos, overtures and an oratorio.

Sir Michael Tippett was born in 1905. He studied at the Royal College of Music, and did not really concentrate on composing until he was in his 30s. During the 1939–45 war he was imprisoned for his pacifist views, but in 1941 he became famous through his oratorio *A Child of Our Time*. From then on he gradually became more successful, and his music now includes several operas and symphonies.

Peter Maxwell Davies and Richard Rodney Bennett are among the composers born later in the 20th century. Peter Maxwell Davies studied at the Royal Manchester College of Music and later in Rome. His music was first

Peter Maxwell Davies, who lives in the Orkneys

Richard Rodney Bennett, who composes a lot of music for children

influenced by serialism (see page 92), and later by medieval music. Richard Rodney Bennett studied at the Royal Academy of Music, and is well known as a composer of film music as well as serious music. Among his best known pieces is his children's opera, *All the King's Men*.

Perhaps the most popular British composer of the 20th century is Benjamin Britten, described in the previous section (page 86).

Questions

1 When was England a leading musical country?
2 Name two composers of this time (see Q.1).
3 Describe the music of the 18th century in England.
4 Which British composer influenced Chopin?
5 Which 19th-century British composers concentrated on church music?
6 How old was Elgar when he became known as a composer?
7 Name two orchestral pieces by Delius.
8 Who wrote the *Fantasia on a Theme of Thomas Tallis*?
9 What piece made Walton well known as a composer?
10 Which 20th-century composer is well known for his film music as well as serious music?

Things to do

1 Elgar's best known piece of music is the *Enigma Variations*, while a well known piece by Vaughan Williams is his *Fantasia on a Theme of Thomas Tallis*. Both these compositions start with a tune which was not written by the composers, but which they use in their piece.

Here is a short tune which you could use when you make up some music of your own in class. Try playing it several different ways: forwards, backwards, inside out (starting with one of the middle bars first), and so on. If you put all your 'variations' together, you will be able to make up a whole piece:

2 Use the information in this chapter to make a poster of British music, from the 16th century to the present day. Include all the composers mentioned, together with their best known compositions.
3 Use a music reference book, such as *The Oxford Junior Companion to Music*, to find out more about the following composers who are briefly mentioned in this chapter. Write down what you find out in your own words:

William Byrd; John Field;
Arthur Sullivan; Hubert Parry.

Schoenberg (1874–1951)

Arnold Schoenberg was born in one of the most famous of 'musical' cities, Vienna. When he was eight he learnt the violin at school, but he had no composition lessons until he was much older.

When his father died, Schoenberg was forced to work as a bank clerk, and could only find time to compose during the evenings. Eventually his hard work impressed a teacher who agreed to give him lessons, and when Schoenberg was 23, his first string quartet was performed.

Two years later, however, Schoenberg's string **sextet** (a piece for six players), *Verklärte Nacht*, was performed, and soon afterwards some of his songs were heard in public. Both these pieces startled the Viennese audiences, because they were so different from the kind of music people were used to. Schoenberg was already showing signs that he was going to be a composer of unusual new music: one of the **avant-garde** composers (see page 94).

By 1913 the public had begun to like Schoenberg's music, and his *Gurrelieder*, for voices and orchestra, was a success. In spite of this, he found that he had to compose ordinary pieces in which he was not interested, and spend time teaching in order to make a living. Two of his pupils, Anton Webern and Alban Berg, later continued to write the kind of new music which Schoenberg was developing.

The composer Arnold Schoenberg with portraits of himself on the wall behind

Anton Webern, a pupil of Schoenberg

Alban Berg, another of Schoenberg's pupils

Schoenberg's manuscrpt of the beginning of his Piano Suite, the first work in which he used serialism throughout

By the time Schoenberg was 30, he began to realize that he had gradually been creating a new type of composition. He decided to spend a lot of time and thought to working out what was to be his new system, with its own 'rules'. By 1923 he had completed this job, and a year later he became professor of composition at the Berlin Academy of Fine Arts. However, in 1933 he was sacked from this post, along with many other Jews at this time.

Schoenberg spent the rest of his life in America, and during this time he sometimes returned to more traditional ways of composing. He taught in various American universities until 1944, when he retired at the age of 70.

Schoenberg's music

The style of music which Schoenberg developed, and which Berg and Webern continued to compose in their own ways, is now called **Twelve-note composition**, or **serial music**. Schoenberg gradually found that his music never seemed to be in the same key, and so he decided to deliberately develop music in no key at all. He did this by composing in **series**.

A series is a musical phrase which contains each of the 12 chromatic notes of the scale in any order. As each note can only be played once, until the whole series is repeated, the music is never in any one key. The order of the series must be the same every time it is repeated, and the only variation Schoenberg allowed was to reverse the series, or turn it upside down, although the notes could have different rhythms. There is an example of a series in *Things to do* on the next page.

Another kind of music which Schoenberg developed was a particular style of singing, called **Sprechgesang**. This means *speech-song*, and is a style of singing in which the singer half sings and half speaks. Schoenberg's most famous example of Sprechgesang is *Pierrot Lunaire*, a piece for 'singer' and five instruments.

Some of Schoenberg's other famous compositions are his *First Chamber Symphony* (which made the audience whistle and bang their seats when it was first performed in 1906!), *Five Orchestral Pieces* (1909), *Erwartung* (a kind of opera) and *Moses and Aaron* (an opera he never finished) in 1930.

A scene from Schoenberg's opera Moses and Aaron

Questions

1　Where was Schoenberg born?
2　How old was Schoenberg when he learnt the violin?

3 Why did Schoenberg become a bank clerk?
4 What effect did the piece *Verklärte Nacht* have on its audience?
5 How did Schoenberg make a living in his 20s?
6 Who were Schoenberg's 'followers', and how did they meet him?
7 What did Schoenberg concentrate on doing between 1915 and 1923?
8 What is a **series** in music?
9 What is *Sprechgesang*?
10 Name some famous compositions by Schoenberg.

Things to do

1a Here is a **tone row** or **series**. In Twelve-note composition the notes of the series must always remain in the same order, unless the series is reversed or inverted (turned upside down). Using a piece of music manuscript paper, see if you can reverse and invert the series below. The first three notes have already been done for you.

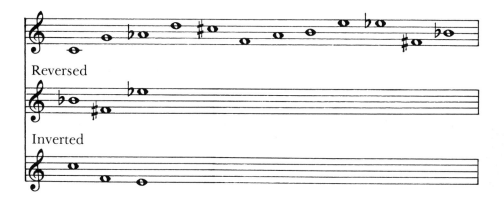

1b Play the series in 1a on a classroom instrument or a piano, and then play it *reversed* and *inverted*. If you do this in a group, you should be able to make up a piece of music, by everyone playing their series at different speeds. Remember, you must always finish a series once you've started it.

2 Make a chart of all the 'rules' of Twelve-note composition. Illustrate it with examples if you can.

3 Schoenberg, like many composers, eventually settled in a country other than his own. Look through this book, or another music reference book (such as *The Oxford Junior Companion to Music*) to find out which other composers did this. Make a list or a chart of this information.

The avant-garde

Avant-garde is an expression which means 'ahead of one's time' (in French it means 'the advance guard'). In music it is now used to describe any composer who is writing in a very advanced or modern way.

There have already been several examples of composers who were once thought to be ahead of their time in this book, and not all are ones who are alive today. For example, when Berlioz was at the Paris Conservatoire in 1824 (see page 47), he was thought of as a revolutionary, and his unusual ideas about composing made him so unpopular with his teachers that it took him five attempts before he won the *Prix de Rome*.

Debussy was another advanced composer in his day (see page 78). He also studied at the Paris Conservatoire, and, like Berlioz, did not always agree with what his teachers expected him to do. When he came back from Rome,

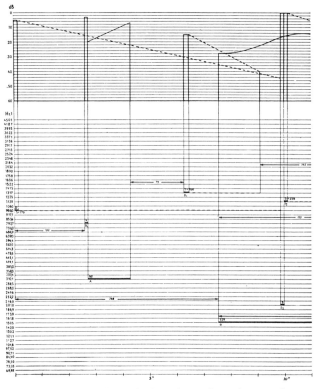

An electronic score. The vertical numbers refer to the tape, the horizontal ones to the duration in seconds

The German composer Karlheinz Stockhausen

after winning the *Prix de Rome*, his compositions were considered so modern and unusual that they were not thought suitable for performance by the Conservatoire. His new ideas were therefore advanced, which is why we can think of him as an avant-garde composer in his own life-time, even though his music might not seem particularly modern or unusual now.

Who are the avant-garde composers of the *20th* century? Perhaps the first was Schoenberg, who by the 1920s had devised a completely new system of music, called Twelve-note

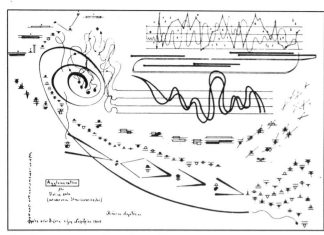

An aleatory score, where players have to decide for themselves what the signs and symbols represent, and in which order to play them

So Stockhausen has always composed new kinds of music, while many other composers of his own age have stuck to more conventional sounds. This is why he is an avant-garde composer.

One of the best known avant-garde composers is John Cage (born 1912). His compositions have been considered so unusual that many people might not even think of them as being music. For example, he developed aleatoric music and called it **indeterminacy**. One of his pieces uses several radio sets tuned to any station, all playing at once.

Perhaps Cage's most famous piece is *4'33"* (meaning four minutes and thirty three seconds). It consists of exactly that amount of

The American composer John Cage

composition (see page 92). He was avant-garde because he was the first composer to write music like this, and lead the way for his followers, Berg and Webern, who developed this new style.

One of the most important types of music to develop during the 20th century is **electronic music**, and the first composers who created this can also be thought of as avant-garde. One of the first composers to make use of electronic music was Karlheinz Stockhausen, a German composer born in 1928. His first compositions consisted of an advanced kind of serial music, which was partly influenced by Webern (see above).

Stockhausen later made use of the idea of chance in music, which allowed the players to have a small say in the way the composition should sound. They could sometimes decide which order to play some musical phrases in, or were encouraged to add notes of their own in the performance. The result has been called **aleatory** music, where each performance can sound different from the previous one.

silence, as the 'pianist' closes the piano lid at the start and opens it again at the end of that time. The 'music' is whatever sounds naturally happened during that time—even the coughs from the audience!

With such a fast development of music in the 20th century, many people may ask, 'What next?' Although some composers, such as Britten (see page 86), have successfully used fairly traditional sounds and notation to create fresh and different music, the avant-garde composers seem to some people to have gone too far. Not all their ideas have been accepted yet, and so much of the new music which we hear today uses conventional notation and ordinary instruments. But perhaps some new form of music which will be popular in the future has still to be discovered. Who knows? In the meantime, we can all enjoy both the music of the present *and* the music of the past.

Questions

1 What does **avant-garde** mean?
2 Give an example of any avant-garde composer of the past.
3 Explain why this composer (Q.2) was avant-garde.
4 How do we know that Debussy was considered avant-garde?
5 Give an example of an avant-garde composer of the 20th century.
6 Explain why this composer (Q.5) is avant-garde.
7 What unusual kind of music did Stockhausen develop?
8 Explain what **aleatory** music is.
9 Which composer developed **indeterminacy**?
10 Give an example of a very unusual avant-garde piece.

Things to do

1 If you ever make up your own music in class, then you can use some of the ideas of avant-garde music yourselves. For example, you can compose aleatory (chance) music, by making a cardboard spinning disc which has different note-values on it and another with different notes (see below). To compose your piece, spin both discs, and wherever the discs stop you write the same note and note length down on manuscript paper. Gradually you can construct a whole piece which has been 'composed' by chance.

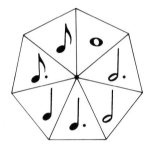 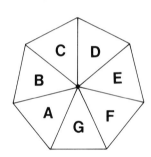

2 In this chapter you can read about John Cage's unusual piece which uses a number of radio sets tuned to any stations. How do you think a piece of music for radio sets used in this way could be written down in 'music'? Try to do this yourself, using whatever system of 'notation' you like.
3 This chapter only tells you about a few avant-garde composers who wrote music in the first half of the 20th century. There are many more who have written music during the last 20 years or less. Use an up to date music reference book (such as *The Oxford Junior Companion to Music*) to try to find out who these composers are. When you have found their names, write about any six of them; try to find composers who we now think of as avant-garde.